May Martin's
SEWING BIBLE

40 years of tips & tricks on how to make your own
fashion, home furnishings & crafts

May Martin's
SEWING BIBLE

40 years of tips & tricks on how to make your own
fashion, home furnishings & crafts

HarperCollins*Publishers*

CONTENTS

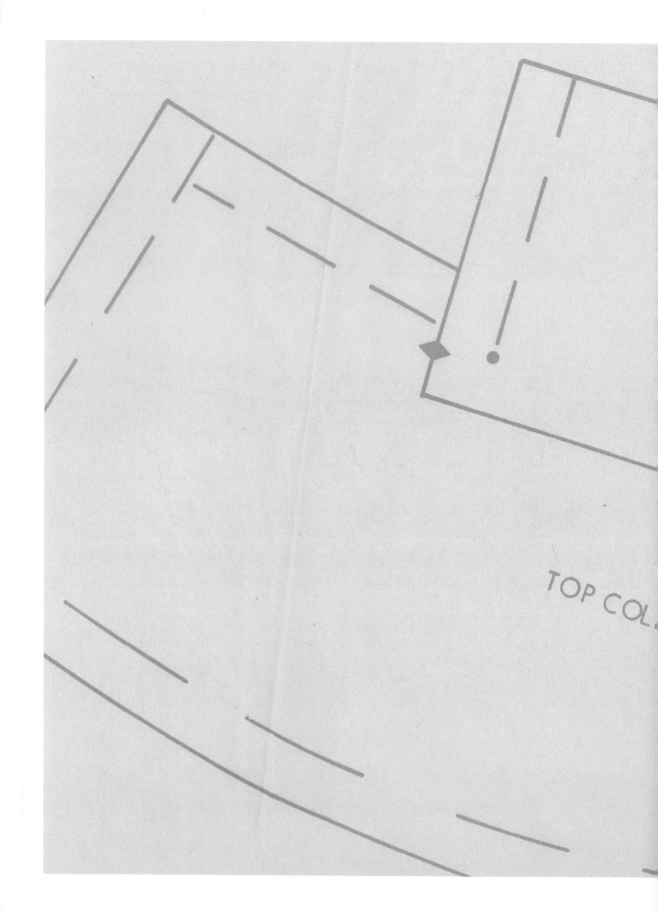

✕

INTRODUCTION

INTRODUCTION

Introduction

I have been a textile tutor for over 40 years and I love my job. I couldn't imagine doing anything more enjoyable. I have a passion for my subject and I love sharing my skills with other people – nothing gives me greater pleasure than helping my students and seeing them progress. At school I was not particularly academic, but I discovered that I could sew and I will never forget the sheer delight of completing my first project, a grey pencil skirt. I trained as a needlework teacher and taught at various schools for several years until my children arrived. I branched into adult education because I could fit it around my family, and I've been teaching students of all ages ever since.

Sewing has become hugely popular again. I've seen it in the growing numbers of students signing on for classes and in the appeal of TV programmes like *The Great British Sewing Bee*, for which I had the privilege of being one of the judges. What was striking about the programme was how well the contestants bonded with each other, and this is something that I've noticed in my own classes. People love to help each other and share their ideas. As a teacher, I find I learn so much from my pupils. I've even included a few tips here that they've shown me, such as the technique for double binding the edge of patchwork to make beautiful mitred corners (see page 106).

In this book, I have tried to gather together some of the tips and tricks I've learned over the years. Along the way, I've discovered different methods of tackling particular techniques that make them easier as well as producing a better finish, and my aim is to share some of the tips that my students have found most helpful. I've begun with the basics – where to sew and what equipment you'll need – and offered advice on the 'raw materials' of a project, from choosing fabric and thread to selecting and laying out a pattern. And I've presented some of the fundamental techniques that are so important in sewing, from how to make different types of seams and hems to such processes as creating your own binding (really easy if you have the right gadget) and forming 'magic' rouleau loops (see pages 104 and 109). At every point, I've tried to demystify the subject for beginners – explaining pattern terms and markings, for instance – while at the same time providing ideas for those with more experience to help enhance their sewing knowledge.

In the second part of the book, I've presented a range of projects to suit varying degrees of skill and ability – beginner, intermediate and more advanced. The skill level is shown at the start of each project. Beginner projects only require straight seams and simple hand stitching; intermediate projects involve curved seams, bound edges and relatively easy fastenings such as drawstrings or centred zips; the more advanced feature facings, interlinings, and matching fabric patterns and may involve assembling several different components. With these I've tried to give a taste of every type of sewing project you might be tempted to try, from craft work – how to make your own bunting or a beautiful puppet theatre, complete with puppets (see pages 136 and 140) – to home furnishings, from a Roman blind to a boxed cushion cover (see pages 184 and 175). There are a number of dressmaking projects too, a range of items for both adults and

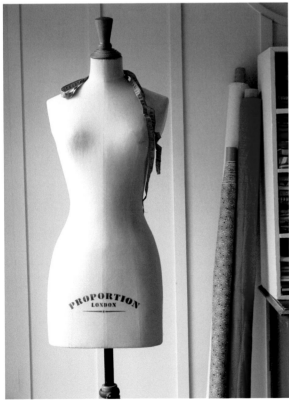

INTRODUCTION

INTRODUCTION

children. These are linked to actual patterns that you can buy – and which you will need for the pattern pieces and full assembly instructions – but you don't have to be restricted to these. My aim has been to try to bring them alive by focusing on particular techniques – such as how to insert an invisible zip or make a smocked panel for a little girl's dress (see pages 227 and 274) – which you can add to your repertoire and use again and again in other projects, building your skills all the time.

It is a privilege to be in a position to reach a wider audience and share what I've learned over the years. It has given me so much pleasure to teach others, helping and guiding them. I hope this book conveys some of that joy so that you in turn will be inspired to begin your own sewing journey.

May Martin

TIPS &
TRICKS

WHERE
TO START

A PLACE TO SEW & THE EQUIPMENT YOU NEED

ESSENTIALS FOR YOUR SEWING SPACE

Once you've identified your sewing space, here are a few basics that I'd recommend:

An electric socket – for plugging in your sewing machine and an extension lead. The power cables on sewing machines are never long enough!

A good lamp – I have an old Anglepoise with a daylight bulb in it – invaluable for ensuring you have enough light to work by, and not just on gloomy winter days.

A comfortable chair – at just the right height for you while you're seated at the sewing machine.

A table – pasting table, folding table, kitchen table, even an ironing board (see page 22) – for cutting out your fabric.

Clear plastic boxes – to store fabrics, threads and haberdashery. I find it invaluable to see instantly where everything is.

ESSENTIAL TOOLS

For your basic sewing kit, you'll need the following items:

Hand-sewing needles – sharps (all-purpose) for hand-sewing, curved needles for craft, crewel (with a long eye) for embroidery. A needle threader is also invaluable.

Pins – dressmaker's and glass-headed.

Thimble – metal, plastic or leather – for protecting the tips of your fingers when you're hand-sewing.

Measures – A standard tape measure is 152cm (60in); an extra-long tape measure (30-cm/120in) is really useful when making curtains. A ruler comes in very handy, too, especially a gridded ruler with angles marked.

Pin cushion – to keep pins handy.

Cutting tools – scissors in different sizes, including dressmaker's shears (25cm/10in), medium embroidery/needlework scissors (13cm/5in), small embroidery scissors (10cm/4in), paper-cutting scissors; and, perhaps not essential but extremely useful, pinking shears, sewing snips, stitch ripper.

Markers – chalk pencils, chalk wheels, air- and water-soluble marker pens (see page 21), dressmaker's chalk, tracing wheel and carbon paper (see opposite).

Tracing or dressmaker's carbon paper and tracing wheel – to copy designs and pattern markings (see opposite).

Coloured tape – to make a sewing guide on the throat plate of the sewing machine, and masking tape.

1. Dressmaker's shears – good for cutting fabric
2. Medium sewing scissors – good for trimming seams and cutting threads.
3. Small scissors – these are useful for clipping corners and cutting details
4. Paper scissors
5. Stitch ripper – really useful for cutting and pulling out threads
6. Tape measure – 150cm (60in)
7. Double-length (300cm/120in) tape measures are now available and are really useful when cutting out curtains and blinds
8. Universal ruler with inch scale
9. Sewing gauge with sliding adjuster – good for measuring seam allowances and hems
10. Small measuring gauge – this has lots of different measurements on the sides
11. Tailor's chalk
12. Tracing wheel
13. Tracing or dressmaker's carbon paper, used with a tracing wheel
14. Retractable pencils – they give a fine line that can be rubbed out with a fabric eraser.
15. Quilter's 6mm (¼ in) tape – helps to guide rows of stitching
16. Coloured tape – useful for putting on the arm of the sewing machine to guide you
17. Pins – dressmaker's
18. Pins – glass-headed
19. Metal thimble
20. Leather thimble
21. Selection of hand sewing needles
22. Needle threader
23. Corner and edge shaper
24. Chopstick – used for turning out tricky corners
25. Safety pins – used for threading elastic or tape into channels.
26. Wrist pin cushion

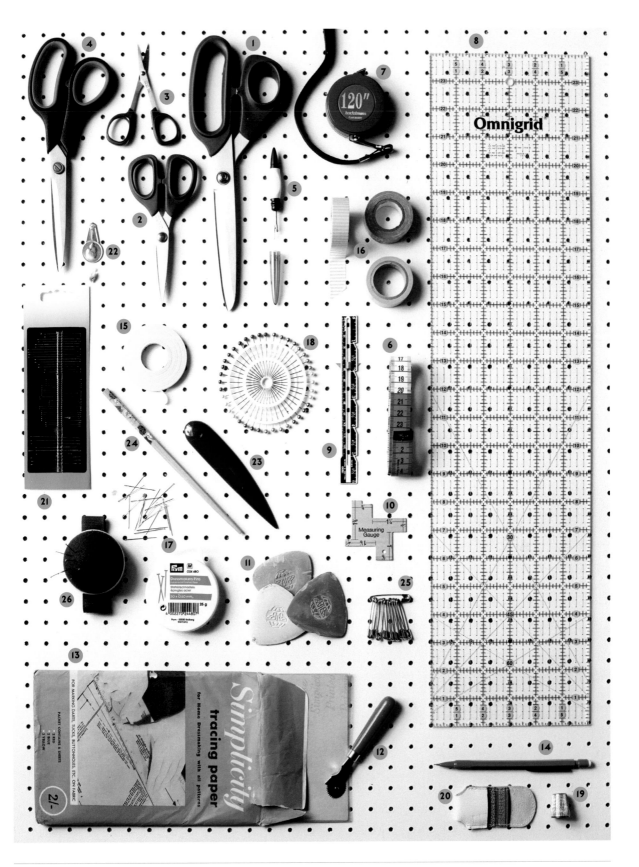

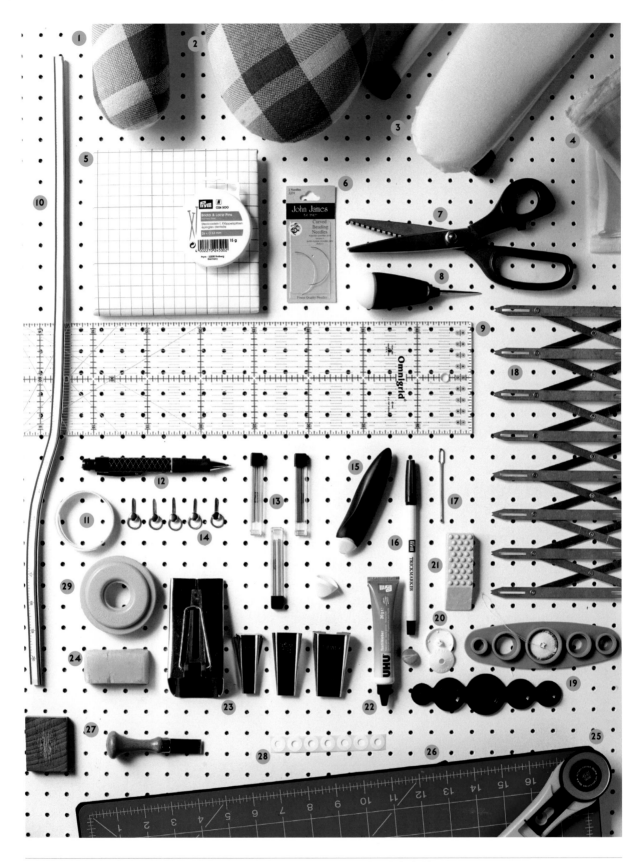

WHERE TO START

1. Seam roll
2. Tailor's ham
3. Sleeve board
4. Pressing muslin
5. Squared pattern paper
6. Curved needles
7. Pinking sheers
8. Awl – good for making holes in card
9. Universal ruler with centimetre scale
10. Flexible ruler – for measuring and marking curves
11. Parcel strapping
12. Chalk cartridge pencil
13. Coloured refills for chalk cartridge pencil
14. Brass rings attached to paper fasteners
15. Chalk-filled tracing wheel
16. Soluble marking pen
17. Bodkin
18. Expanding gauge – excellent for spacing buttonholes, pleats and more
19. Button press
20. Button for covering
21. Fabric rubber
22. Fabric glue
23. Tape and binding makers. These are handy gadgets and come in different sizes; the fabric is threaded through and the edges are rolled under to form bias or straight binding.
24. Beeswax – before doing any hand sewing, run the thread through the wax; this will prevent it from tangling and will make it stronger.
25. Rotary cutter – this is a specialist cutter with a rotary blade that can cut through several layers of fabric at once. Use only with its special mat and ruler. Very useful for cutting parallel trims, bias strips, pieces for patchwork and much more.
26. Cutting mat
27. Chisel and block to cut buttonholes
28. Hole reinforcements
29. Weights

USEFUL ADDITIONS TO YOUR KIT

The following items, while not essential, can come in very handy for different projects:

Bodkin –for pulling elastic through a casing.

Bridal and lace pins – finer pins for using with delicate fabrics and projects such as wedding dresses.

Sewing gauge – great for spacing buttons and buttonholes without measuring.

Flexible curve ruler – very useful for marking curves (such as for the Man's Apron on page 204).

Rotary cutter – especially useful for quilting, but great for cutting any straight edge with the aid of a ruler and cutting mat.

Craft hole punch – for making holes in leather and card.

Bias binding and tape maker – these come in different sizes and are really useful for making straight or bias tape (see page 104).

Beeswax – waxing thread prevents tangling.

Fabric eraser – for rubbing out marks on cloth.

SEWING MACHINE

It goes without say that, for most sewing projects, a sewing machine is vital, and I've devoted a whole section to it – see pages 54–73.

OVERLOCKER

An overlocker is a much more specialised piece of equipment, but it creates a really professional finish to garments – see pages 74–79 for further details.

IRON & IRONING BOARD

An iron and ironing board are needed at every stage of a sewing project, so it's a good idea to set them up in a convenient location before you start. The ironing board comes in handy as an extra work surface, too. Put two ironing boards together with a board on the top and you have an adjustable-height work surface!

Other useful pressing aids are:

A seam roll – this is a padded tube, great for pressing seams inside sleeves and trouser. The roll holds the seam edges away when pressing so the indents don't occur. For a bargain alternative, go to your local fabric shop and pick up a tube from the middle of a roll of fabric. Wrap it in a thin towel – and hey presto, you have a seam roll! The longer length of this tube is excellent for pressing long seams such as the table runner on page 120. You could even use a tube of cardboard from inside a roll of kitchen paper or plastic food wrap.

Sleeve boards – a sleeve board is like a mini ironing board on legs – it stands on your ironing board and is great for pressing tubes such as sleeves and trouser seams. They are also useful when pressing children's clothes,

which have small, fiddly seams and shaping.

Brown paper, printer paper, sugar paper – cut into strips and position under your seam allowances to prevent them from imprinting on the right side of the garment.

Tailor's ham – really useful for pressing darts, panels and shaping, as they mimic the contour of the body.

Needleboard: These are boards with rows of needles that stand up and position themselves in the pile of the fabric, preventing flattening of the pile. They are great for pressing fabrics with a pile. For an effective alternative, place a spare piece of the fabric pile side up on the ironing board, then put your garment pile side down on top and press.

Pressing cloth – a pressing cloth is a fine piece of muslin that you lay on top of your fabric. When dry, it protects the fabric while you iron; when dampened, it aids pressing and shrinking.

Pressing mat – a portable padded mat that can be placed to protect and pad any work surface so that you can press anywhere.

TAILOR'S DUMMY

While not essential, tailor's dummies are a great tool for working on and fitting a garment – particularly for checking the back view or if you're making an item of clothing for someone else. I had my first tailor's dummy 40 years ago. A friend of my mum's gave her to me and I called her Gladys. She travelled with us from house to house until eventually she rusted and fell apart. A couple of years ago, I decided to replace her; I assembled the new mannequin in my studio and started to customise her to my shape. As I worked, I chatted to her. My

WHERE TO START

husband could hear me talking and asked if I had a visitor!

Tailor's dummies come in different sizes and are adjustable. When choosing one to buy, it's best to go for a model that is either exactly your size or slightly smaller as you can add layers, as I'll explain here. My weight fluctuates and it is marvellous to be able to peel off a layer from my dummy when I lose a few pounds!

Customising a tailor's dummy

Tailor's dummies are made up of expandable sections with adjustment wheels that can be operated to increase or decrease the gaps between the sections and hence the overall size. Dummies come classically proportioned, too, so may need some adjustment – mine certainly did! For the best results, it's a good idea to customise the dummy to fit you exactly. As well as adjusting the individual sections of the dummy, I use padding to create a more lifelike outline.

1. First take your measurements – chest, waist and hips – then adjust the wheels on the expandable sections until they are as near as possible to your size.

2. Find a bra that fits you really well and pad the cups. Put the bra on the dummy and check that the bust is in the right place. Measure from your shoulder to the bust point, then loosen or tighten the straps on the bra to match.

3. Gradually bind the body of the dummy with 70g (2oz) wadding, adding those extra layers of flesh that determine the shape of our bodies. Measure at every stage as you do this, stopping when the dummy matches your measurements. This is a really flexible way of changing the shape of your dummy and you can add more in one area if required.

4. Now take some stockinette – the stretchy tubular cotton fabric you use to cover foam for upholstery projects – and cut a 1.5m (1⅝yd) length. Unscrew the neck of your dummy, put the stockinette tube over the top of the dummy and pull it down over the body. Tuck the stockinette into the neck and tighten the neck screw. Pull the fabric right down and tie under the body of the dummy.

Stockinette is quite flimsy, however, so I bought a close-fitting cheap T-shirt and put this on as the top layer. I then tried one of my dresses on the dummy to check for fit. Perfect! (And no, she hasn't got a name yet!)

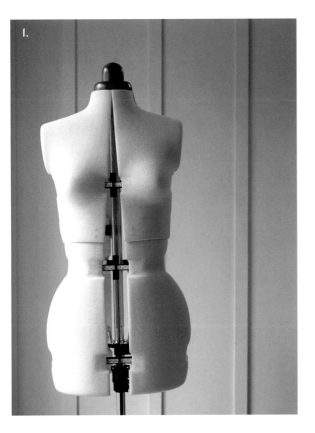

1.

2.

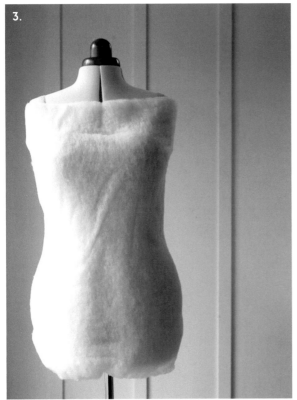

3.

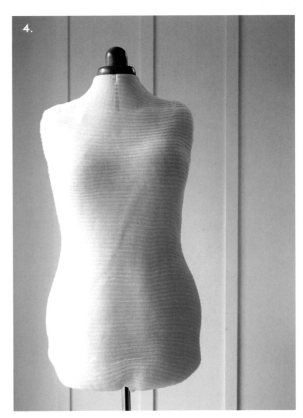

4.

WHERE TO START

WHERE TO START

THE RAW MATERIALS

FABRIC FOR CRAFT OR HOME-FURNISHING PROJECTS

For my craft projects you'll see I've mostly used cotton, for its weight and texture as well as its wide colour range, but you can use any fabric you like, within reason, as long as you sew together fabrics of a similar weight where more than one is needed. Cotton is also ideal for making curtains, blinds or other home furnishings, especially if you're just starting out. My students buy whatever catches their eye and whatever they think will best fit their overall colour scheme. The main thing to bear in mind is pattern matching, which I explain in detail in the section on making curtains (see page 190).

CHOOSING FABRIC FOR YOUR DRESSMAKING PROJECT

My students frequently ask my advice when it comes to selecting fabric for a dressmaking project, so here are a few pointers to help you make your choice.

First purchase your pattern and look at the back of the envelope for fabric recommendations and quantities (see page 36). Decide whether your garment is going to be worn in the winter or the summer – this will determine the weight of the fabric and the sort of colours to go for.

Fabrics are usually grouped in weights: lighter-weight cottons and silks and heavier-weight woollens. Information about the fabric is usually given on the end of the roll: the fabric type, width and content (the proportion of natural and synthetic fibres), along with care instructions. If you are making clothes for small children or are in constant contact with small children and their sticky fingers, it's best to go for a washable fabric – you don't want a huge dry-cleaning bill!

When you're shopping for fabric, apart from your paper pattern and what's written on the end of the roll, it's your eyes and hands that are your best tools. Cast your eyes along the shelves, homing in on colours or patterns that appeal. Now use your hands – this is where you will gain the most information about a piece of cloth. These are the important factors to bear in mind:

Comfort: Feel the cloth: is it rough to the touch? If so, it may benefit from a lining so that it does not scratch your skin.

Modesty: When you hold the fabric up, can you see the outline of your hand through it? If so, other people will be able to see your silhouette through the fabric when you stand against the light! You will either need to line the sections of your garment before sewing them together or drop in a loose lining.

Creasability: Take a small amount of the cloth in your hand and squeeze it gently. How well does it bounce back? If it retains a crease when you crush it with your fingers, it will crease when you wear it.

Stability: Is the end of the fabric on the roll unravelling? If so, the cloth will fray like fury and may be tricky to handle.

Mobility: Does the fabric move about if you drape a couple of metres over your arm? This could be a good thing if your pattern requires drape in the design. It could be a nightmare if the fabric is so mobile that it stretches in every direction!

Another factor to bear in mind when choosing fabric is whether it has a nap – a slightly raised or textured surface that looks different depending on which way up the fabric is. Fabrics with a nap need to be cut out with pattern pieces all laid in the same direction (see page 39). How do you tell if a fabric has a nap? Take a length of the fabric and fold it back side by side against a piece going in the other direction. If there is a difference in sheen or colour, you will need to position pattern pieces in one direction. If in any doubt, treat as a napped fabric. There is nothing more heart-breaking than nearing completion of a garment and noticing that a section is not quite right. Other factors to bear in mind are:

Pile: Velvet and corduroy both have an obvious pile, which can be challenging to sew as it creeps on seams (one bit walking on top of another). As with any fabric with a nap, it needs to be cut out with all the pieces of the garment lying in the same direction.

Sheen: Silk, satin and other fabrics with a sheen all need to be handled with care and pattern pieces cut out in the same direction.

Pattern: Does the fabric have a distinctive pattern? If so, you may need to allow more fabric as you'll need to consider the positioning of the paper pattern on the fabric when you cut out your garment (see pages 39 and 269). Just as you would for fabric with a nap, you will also need to position your paper pattern with the pieces all laying in the same direction.

If you're making a garment out of a heavier-weight fabric, especially one with a rough texture such as wool, then it's best to line it. Lining also gives a better drape to a garment, and you'll see I've suggested inserting one in my Pencil Skirt on page 230. For either purpose, you'd select lining made from a silky polyester or acetate. Garment pieces can also be underlined – where you attach lining to individual sections of a garment before sewing it together, as I've done for the Boned Bodice on page 240. Polyester and cotton curtain lining is ideal for use in craft projects, as it does not shrink or change shape when it is washed. I have used it in the the Patchwork Place Mat and Christmas Stocking (see pages 128 and 154). For curtains, I prefer to use cotton lining.

"WHEN YOU'RE shopping *for Fabric,* it's your *eyes and hands* THAT ARE YOUR Best Tools."

WHERE TO START

INTERFACING

Interfacing is used to add body to a garment to give firmness and stability. It is applied to the wrong side of certain parts of the garment during construction, typically collars, cuffs and bands where buttonholes are worked. Interfacing should not overpower or change the natural character of a fabric; it should support and enhance without making it rigid.

Many different types of interfacing are available, from ultra-fine for use in dressmaking to heavyweight buckram for crafts and curtain headings, so how do you choose the right kind for your fabric? It's best to select a similar weight of interfacing to the fabric you are using – feel the texture and drape of the interfacing compared with that of the main fabric. If you can, test a small piece tacked or fused on to your fabric. When there is a choice between a heavier or a lighter weight of interfacing, choose the latter. It is possible to add more than one layer of lighter-weight interfacing.

Types of interfacing

There are three main types of interfacing:

Non-woven: This type is made from bonded fibres and has a felt-like appearance. It has no grain line and can be cut out in any direction.

Woven: This has a grain line and needs to be cut out with the grain going in exactly the same direction as the garment piece to which it will be attached,. The garment will hang better as a result

Knitted: This type of interfacing has a knitted structure that enables it to stretch with the garment.

All of the above types can be purchased in sew-in and fusible (iron-on) forms:

Sew-in: This is good to use on fabric with a pile or a texture that may not be able to cope with the hot iron required to melt the glue on fusible interfacing. It needs to be cut out and tacked onto the wrong side of the piece that it is supporting. It is caught into the seams during construction.

Fusible: Fusible interfacing is very convenient, as you effectively 'glue' it on to the parts of the garment that need reinforcement without needing to tack it in place. Here are some basic instructions for applying it:

1. Cut out the interfacing using the pattern piece of the shape to be stiffened.

2. Trim most of the seam allowance from the edge of the piece. This will reduce bulk during construction.

3. Place the garment piece with the wrong side facing you. Position the piece of interfacing glue side down on top of the fabric.

4. Press into position. Lift the iron up and down, working from the centre of the interfacing outwards. It will take a few seconds in each place for the glue to melt.

Top Tip

Fusible interfacing needs to be handled with care. I put an oven liner on the ironing board to protect it from the sticky deposits that sometimes escape from the interfacing when I'm ironing it into position.

THREAD

Having selected your fabric, you'll then need to choose a reel or two of thread to go with it. Thread comes in varying thicknesses and types and is graded: the higher the number, the finer the thread. Standard sewing thread is size 50 and will suit most projects.

With a rainbow of different hues to choose from, selecting the right colour can be tricky: if in doubt, choose a shade darker than your project. I'm always amazed, however, at how well certain neutral shades go with almost any colour of fabric. My quilting friends swear by shades of grey thread, as they blend with a multitude of coloured fabrics.

Buying good quality and new

It's important to buy good-quality thread. If the thread has no details of any kind on the end of the spool, it is probably inferior quality. If you can, examine a strand of thread against a piece of white paper. If it looks fluffy, it is probably a cheaper type of thread made with insufficient twist so the fibres do not hold together and therefore it will tend to break and deposit fluff between the tension discs of your sewing machine.

Granny's sewing basket is not the best place to go hunting for cotton reels. Thread is one of the items of haberdashery that does not age well. Over time it deteriorates, losing elasticity and becoming brittle so that it breaks easily. Sadly, old thread is only good for tacking.

Types of thread

In the sewing projects you'll see that I've recommended reels of all-purpose sewing thread. Designed to be used on a domestic sewing machine, these come in different fibre types, so you can find one to suit most projects and fabrics.

Cotton: Cotton thread has little or no give and hence is best used on stable or natural fibres. If you use it to sew knitted fabrics, such as cotton jersey, your machine needle may skip and the thread may break.

Polyester: This type of thread has strength and elasticity. It won't fade or shrink in the wash. Most polyester thread has a silicone coating that helps it glide through the machine and the fabric. Ideal for sewing knitted fabrics.

Cotton-wrapped polyester: This thread has the elasticity of polyester and the heat resistance of cotton. It can be used on both knitted and woven fabrics.

Silk: A beautiful lustrous thread, great for tailoring as it moulds when pressed. The stitches sink into the seam lines and become invisible.

Rayon: This type of thread was originally developed as a cheaper alternative to silk. Like silk, it has a sheen and produces fine stitching. Although not as strong as polyester or cotton thread, it is good for sewing embroidery and more delicate fabrics.

NOTIONS

These are all the additional items you will need to finish your garment – zips, buttons, binding, decorative trims and braids etc. Once you have found the fabric that you think suits your project, you can ask an assistant for guidance. A good fabric shop will be able to help you choose the right interfacing and all those little bits and pieces that will aid successful garment completion.

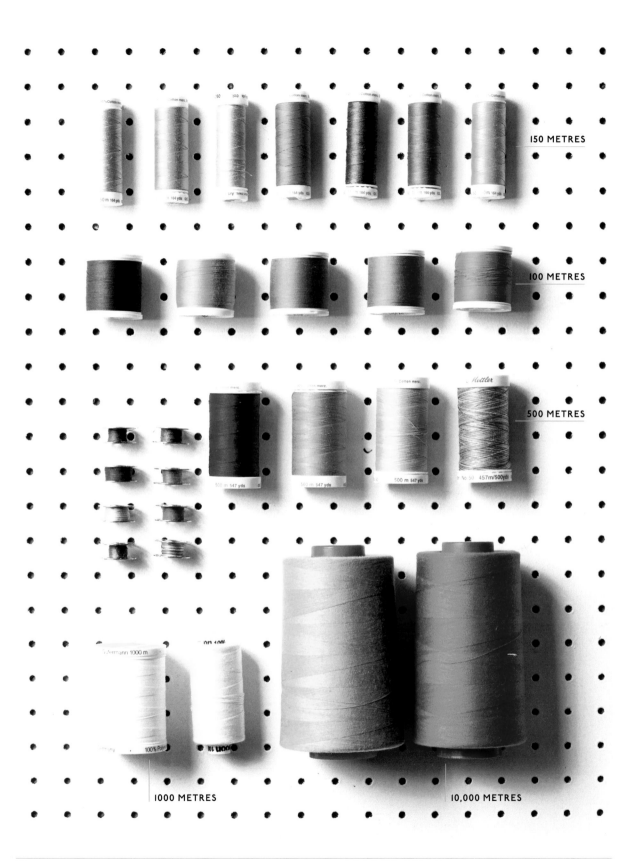

150 METRES

100 METRES

500 METRES

1000 METRES

10,000 METRES

WHERE TO START

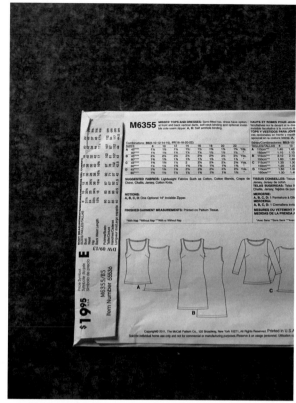

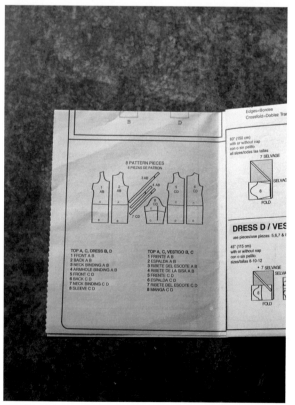

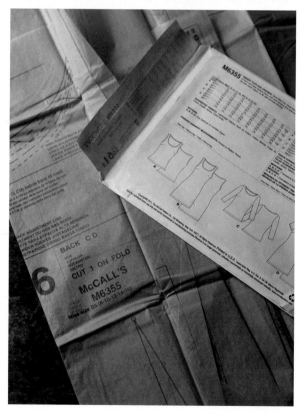

PAPER PATTERNS

There are many different brands of paper pattern and the choice available is huge, not just for dressmaking but for craft and home-furnishing projects too. Once you've chosen your pattern, everything else will fall into place as the pattern not only provides the template for your dressmaking or other project, but offers advice on the type of fabric to choose, along with all the other bits and pieces you'll need.

CHOOSING A PATTERN FOR YOUR DRESSMAKING PROJECT

When I first started sewing, I loved popping into my local fabric shop to perch on a stool at what was called the 'pattern bar' and flick through the pages of various catalogues. It was wonderful to look through the many styles on offer and make my choice. Today I tend to use the internet and a site specialising in paper patterns. Seated by my computer, instead of a pattern bar, I explore the many pages of patterns on view before making my choice. My students often ask me how to choose their first project. Build your skills gradually, is what I advise them, and choose one within your capabilities. Dressmaking takes you on a voyage of discovery and there are many techniques to learn. I am there in the class to guide my students and help them on their journey. Here are a few pointers that I would give anyone just beginning:

1. Choose a simple style: the simpler the style, the quicker you will construct and finish the project.

2. Look for a pattern described by the manufacturer as easy.

3. Look at the line drawing of the design on the back of the pattern. A very basic indication of the degree of difficulty is the number of lines or details on the style diagram. The more lines on the drawing, the greater the number of pieces and therefore construction details.

4. For your first project, pick a style with just a few design features or lines on the drawing of the garment. The Pencil Skirt (page 230) is a simple yet stylish design that would made a good first project. It has a front piece, two back pieces and a waistband. You will learn how to make darts, construct and neaten seams, how to put in a zip, attach a waistband and finish a hem. An excellent place to start.

Following a pattern

Once you've selected your pattern, work with a friend or classmate to take body measurements. Compare these measurements to those on the pattern envelope, and don't be alarmed! You will probably be a larger size than you would be in a ready-made garment. The next step is getting to grips with the pattern itself. A paper pattern is full of useful information but navigating your way through all the detail can seem a little bewildering at first, especially as each pattern covers a range of sizes and as well as various versions of the same garment. Here is a short guide.

Pattern envelope

The front of the envelope gives the pattern number, make and size (or range of sizes). There will be a photo or sketches of the garment showing the different versions or 'views', each marked with a letter (A, B, C, etc).

The back of the envelope includes the following:

✕ A line drawing (or drawings) of the garment showing the design features – really helpful for assessing the level of difficulty of the pattern.

✕ A description of the garment(s), including the principal features (darts, waistband, zip closure, etc.).

✕ A list of fabrics that would be suitable for the project and whether this includes fabric with a nap (see page 28).

✕ A list of 'notions' or extra items you need to complete your garment – zip, buttons, hooks and eyes, etc.

✕ A chart with garment size (or age for children's clothes) along the top and quantity of fabric in different widths underneath.

✕ On the pattern flap there is a chart with size and body measurements.

✕ Occasionally there may be symbols to give you an idea of suitability for certain figure shapes:

The Hourglass Equally balanced on top and bottom, with a trim waist

The Inverted Triangle large bust and/or broad shoulders with narrow hips

The Rectangle balanced on top and bottom but boxy, with little or no waist or definition

The Triangle Small bust and/ or narrow shoulders with full hips and/ or thighs

You will find paper pattern pieces printed and joined together on sheets of tissue. There will be a couple of instruction sheets with line drawings of the garment, suggested layouts of the pattern for different fabric widths, and instructions for constructing the garment.

On the first instruction sheet you'll see a list of pattern pieces needed for each view featured on the front of the envelope. Ring the 'view' you are making and highlight the pattern pieces you need. Find the pattern layout for your width of fabric and style and highlight the heading, then select and carefully cut out the pattern pieces you need (see also 'Pin-fitting a paper pattern' on page 44).

Pattern markings

A paper pattern is like a jigsaw puzzle. All the pieces will fit together beautifully to produce a wonderful end result, but to achieve this you need to lay each piece out in the optimum way, laying them along the grain line of the fabric as instructed and using them to cut out your fabric carefully and accurately. Some of the markings you'll find on your pattern pieces are shown opposite. It's important to understand them before you start cutting out., so read the explanation of each marking on page 38. Older paper patterns may have perforations to mark details. Modern patterns tend to have the markings printed on.

Meaning	Perforated (older patterns)	Printed (modern patterns)
Lay to the fold	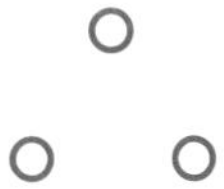	
Straight of grain		
Fitting line of seam allowance		
Notches or balance marks		
Darts		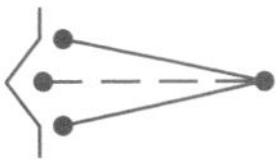
Centre or fold lines		
Pleats	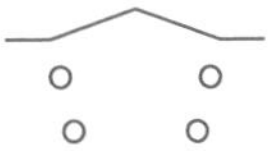	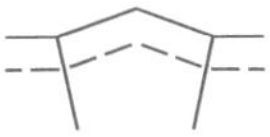
Button and buttonhole positions		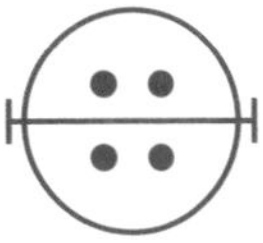
Bust, waist and hip line		

Lay to the fold: When a pattern piece has one of these markings on the edge, that edge should be placed on a folded edge of fabric. This is usually created by folding the fabric in half lengthways so that the selvedges meet.

Straight of grain: This line should lie along the grain line of the fabric (see opposite). Usually the grain line of the pattern piece is positioned parallel to the selvedge, with each pointed end of the line the same distance from the selvedge.

Fitting line or seam allowance: This line is usually situated 1.5cm (⅝in) from the edge of the pattern. It indicates where the seam is to be sewn and hence where you join your fabric pieces together.

Notches or balance marks: These help you to position one piece of fabric at exactly the right point on another. They are single, double or triple. Cut out double or triple notches as a single unit and always cut notches outwards, never inwards, or you will lose some of your seam allowance.

Darts: These are the marks on the pattern piece indicating where a dart is positioned; they need to be marked with tailor's tacks (see page 42).

Centre line or fold lines: These are the lines on the garment where the centre front aligns with another part of the garment. I often put a tiny clip at either end of the line.

Pleats: These are markings indicating where pleats should be made; they need to be marked with tailor's tacks.

Button and buttonhole positions: These mark where to sew a button or make a buttonhole.

Bust, waist or hip line: This mark indicates the position of the bust, waist or hips on a garment.

LAYING THE PAPER PATTERN ALONG THE GRAIN

When you put on a sweater, you probably notice how it's really stretchy when you pull it across your body but less so when you pull it down. The same applies to fabric in general, whether the structure is woven or knitted, like the cotton jersey of a T-shirt. Fabric is always stronger and more stable along the lengthways grain, or 'warp' thread in woven fabric. For this reason, pattern pieces need to be laid out in relation to the grain of the fabric, whether it's woven or knitted, the main sections being laid parallel with the grain line.

WOVEN FABRIC

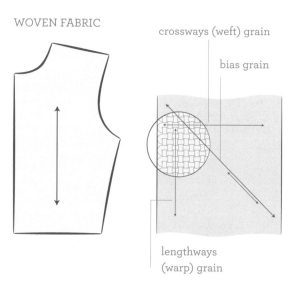

crossways (weft) grain

bias grain

lengthways (warp) grain

KNITTED FABRIC

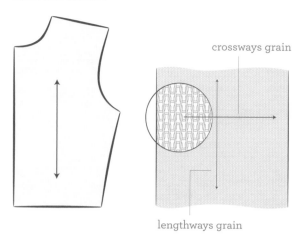

crossways grain

lengthways grain

Laying out a paper pattern on fabric without a nap or pattern

On plain fabric without a nap or pattern, the pattern pieces do not all have to lie in the same direction. To ensure that the pattern piece is placed on the straight grain, measure from the selvedge to the straight grain line on the pattern in at least two places.

Laying out a paper pattern on fabric with a nap or pattern

If you're using fabric with a nap (see page 28), the pieces all need to run in one direction, with the main sections (i.e. not necessarily the facings) all positioned the same way up. If you're using patterned fabric, it's important to ensure that the pattern flows all the way around the garment and hence pattern pieces are matched at the front (see page 236) and on the side seams.

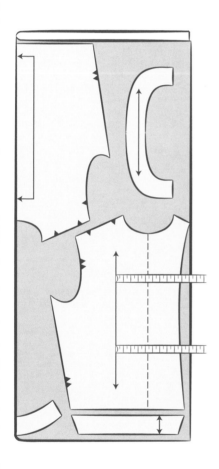

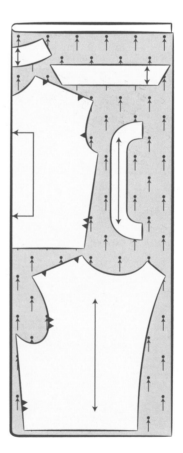

"Always *Pattern Match* at the CENTRE FRONT *of a garment,* EVEN IF YOU CAN'T MATCH OTHER SEAMS."

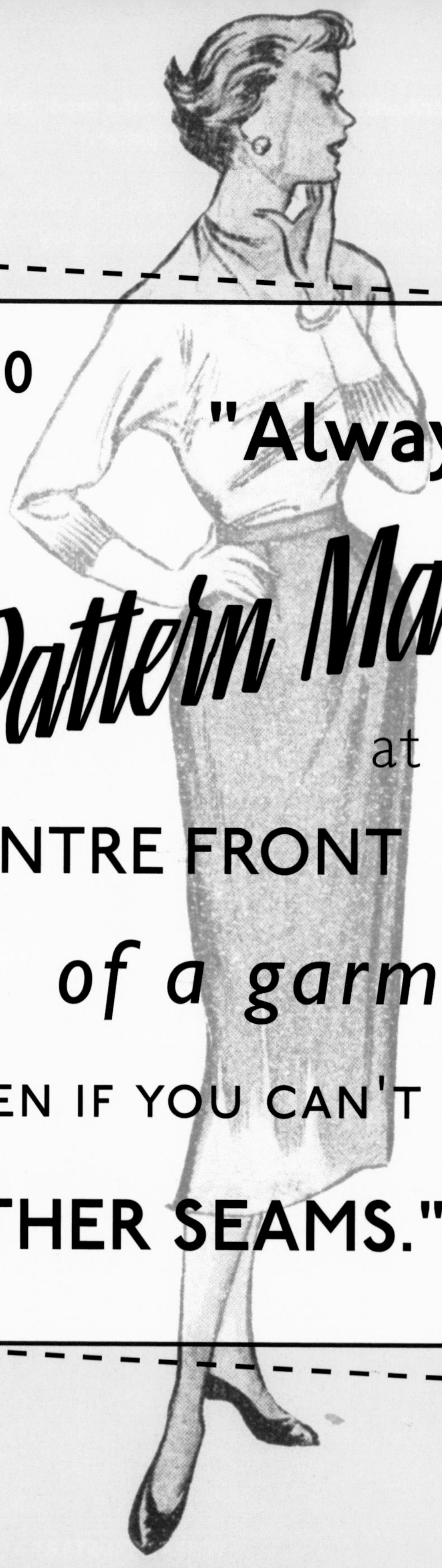

Skirt only

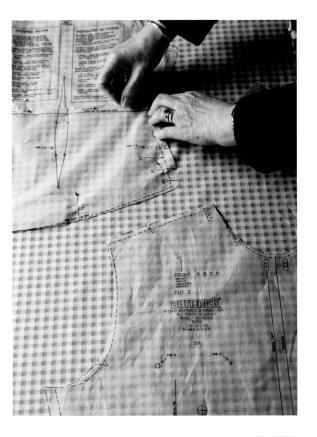

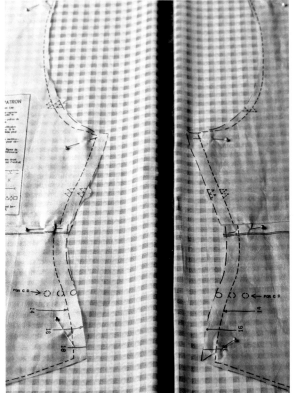

STRAIGHTENING THE EDGE OF THE FABRIC

Before laying out the pattern pieces, it's important to check that your fabric is lying flat and straight. When you fold fabric in half, always ensure that the selvedges are aligned. Straightening the edge of the fabric is good practice, too, as it's all too easy to cut out two pieces of a garment from a double layer of fabric only to find that the piece underneath is shorter because the edges weren't level. When I trained, my tutors were very keen for us to pull out a weft thread across our fabric which we then used as a guide for cutting the end of the fabric in a straight line. I still do this occasionally but have developed other ways for straightening the edge of the fabric.

Table edge

1. Lay your fabric in a single layer along a table – or a similar surface with a right-angle at the end – with the selvedge parallel with the edge of the table and the end of the fabric overlapping the end of the table.

2. Anchor the cloth in position. I use big clothes pegs, but tins or jam jars weighted with sand would be equally effective.

3. Run a triangular piece of dressmaker's chalk along the end of the fabric where it overlaps the edge of the table. You will have a dead-straight line!

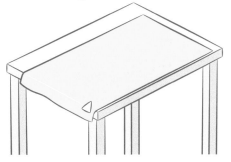

Gridded ruler

1. Lay out your fabric, then position the ruler so that one of the grid lines aligns with the selvedge.

2. Draw a line at right-angles to the selvedge.

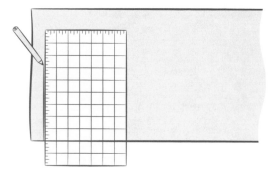

3. If your ruler is not long enough to extend across the whole width of the fabric, you can move it further along the line you've drawn and continue the line across the fabric.

TRANSFERRING PATTERN MARKINGS ONTO FABRIC

Having cut out your pattern pieces and laid them out on the fabric, you'll need to transfer the relevant markings onto your fabric to ensure that you match up the pattern pieces accurately and insert details such as darts or pockets in exactly the right place. There are various techniques for doing this.

Tracing wheel and dressmaker's carbon (tracing) paper

A traditional method for transferring pattern markings to fabric, this is ideal for marking stitching, grain and placement lines (such as for pockets and buttonholes) both quickly and accurately. I also use it to transfer the outline of a multi-size pattern, particularly when making children's clothes as it means you don't have to cut up the pattern and can keep it intact to use again for the next size up as they grow.

The tracing wheel has a serrated edge that punctures the carbon paper and leaves a row of dots on your fabric. The carbon comes in different colours – beware using bright pink on white fabric as it may not come off! Likewise, be gentle when marking darts or details on the middle of the garment piece, where they will be more visible. in case the markings are too firmly printed and difficult to rub off.

How to use

1. Before using dressmaker's carbon paper on your garment fabric, test the different-coloured papers on a scrap of cloth.

2. Check that the tracing wheel does not damage the fabric.

3. Place the dressmaker's carbon paper carbon side up on your work surface. Position your double layer of fabric with the paper pattern attached on top of the tracing paper.

4. Using the wheel, gently trace the detail lines – using a ruler along any straight lines – checking that all are marked.

5. Flip the fabric over, having first removed the paper pattern, and place the dressmaker's carbon paper under the garment, carbon side up. Use the lines you have just made to transfer markings to the other side of the fabric.

TAILOR'S TACKS

This is a method of marking and transferring key points, particularly darts, tucks, and seam lines, from a paper pattern onto fabric –

usually a double layer. It's best to use a double thickness of thread and in a colour that will show up on the fabric, although I wouldn't advise using a dark thread on light fabric as it will leave fibres on your cloth that may not come out! When marking a crowded area, use different colours of thread – for tucks that are close together or overlap, for example. It will be easier to see individual tucks if a different colour is used for each one.

Marking darts and single dots on the pattern

1. Pick up the first spot and leave a tail 2.5cm (1in) long (diagram a).

2. Pick up the spot again and create a 2.5cm (1in) loop, then cut the thread, leaving another tail 2.5cm (1in) long. Repeat for the other two spots (diagrams b and c).

3. Remove the pattern carefully without cutting the loops (see tip below). Gently pull the two layers of fabric apart slightly and snip the threads in between the two layers.

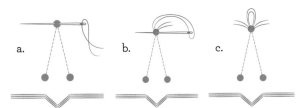

a.   b.   c.

Transferring lines

1. To transfer lines from a pattern to fabric, take a series of looped tacking stitches through the pattern and fabric. Make a loop every other stitch, making sure the loops are at least 2.5cm (1in) long.

2. Lift the pattern off carefully. Gently separate the two layers of fabric and cut the threads in between.

Top Tip

I use hole reinforcements on my paper pattern (see photo) to prevent it from tearing when I pull my pattern off the tailor's tacks. I do not cut through the loops on top of the paper pattern, as these help to keep the layers of fabric anchored when you're separating them for snipping the threads in between.

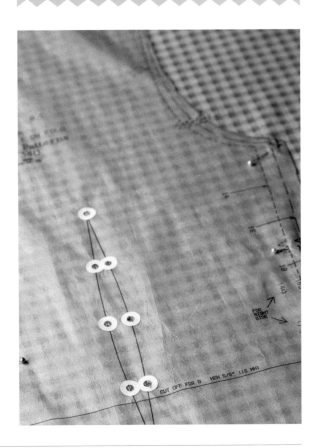

WHERE TO START

CLIPPING DETAIL LINES

It can be difficult to mark a line accurately using tailor's tacks. Equally, a tracing wheel may not be suitable for your fabric if it's delicate or could be permanently marked by the carbon paper. In such cases, an alternative is to make the tiniest clip with the tips of a really sharp pair of scissors at each end of each centre front and fold lines.

DRESSMAKER'S CHALK & MARKER PENS

Dressmaker's chalk is ideal for marking fabric. I use chalk triangles when marking soft furnishings and straightening the edge of fabric (see page 41). A chalk wheel or pencil is perfect for marking finer details, as is a retractable pencil. Marker pens are designed to be used with fabric, but they can be dangerous, in my view. The markings are supposed to be air or water soluble, but once you place a hot iron on top of them, they become permanent! Great care and awareness are needed if you wish to use one.

PIN-FITTING A PAPER PATTERN

This is a great way of testing the fit of your paper pattern. You will get a really good idea about the fit of your chosen style. It is easier if you work with a friend or fellow student in class. It's also best to fit the pattern over a close-fitting T-shirt.

1. Measure your body – bust, waist, hips and back length (photos 1 and 2).

2. Look at the flap on the pattern envelope (see page 35) and find the size closest to your measurements.

3. Referring to the pattern envelope, pull out all the pattern pieces you will need for the style you have chosen.

4. If the pattern is multi-size, it may be helpful to go over the pattern outline in your size using a coloured felt pen. It can be confusing when you have several rows of dots and dashes.

5. Cut out your pattern pieces. Following the details on the paper pattern, pin together darts and join panels together along the seams.

6. Put your arm through the sleeve hole – it may be easier to pin the shoulder seam once you are in!

7. Pin the paper pattern to your centre front and back (photos 3 and 4).

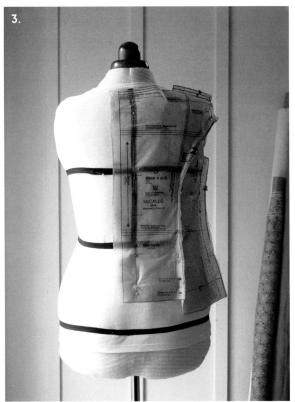

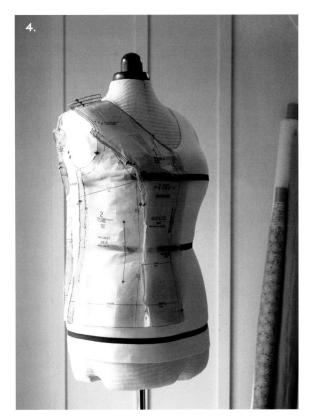

45

WHERE TO START

ALTERING A PAPER PATTERN

Paper patterns can be altered in numerous different ways – there are whole books on them! Here are a couple of very basic alterations that you can do.

Lengthening or shortening a paper pattern

Whether lengthening or shortening a pattern piece, first draw a coloured line in felt-tip pen at right-angles to the lengthening/shortening line and parallel with the grain line.

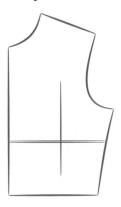

When you've made the alteration to the pattern, put a ruler across the gap to make sure that the line you've drawn still lines up on either side.

To lengthen a pattern piece, cut through the lengthening/shortening line and separate the two pieces of the pattern by the required amount. Place some paper behind the gap and tape in place using masking tape.

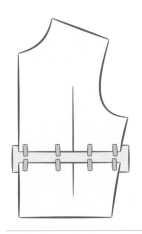

(Sellotape will melt when you iron your pattern pieces!)

To shorten a pattern piece, crease along the lengthening/shortening line and fold away the excess, making a tuck in the paper pattern measuring half the amount to be shortened.

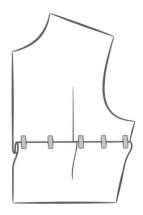

A generous seam allowance!

While it's easy enough to cut away any excess on pattern pieces, adding to them once you've cut them out isn't so easy, of course. That's why I always cut out side seams with a larger seam allowance of 2.5cm (1in) as a security blanket – just in case the pattern proves a bit too snug!

MAKING A TOILE

When making a really special garment or a style for the first time, I often go a step further and make a toile. This is a test garment made from the pattern pieces cut out first in calico, curtain lining or sheeting. You get a much better idea of how the garment will fit, as the fabric follows the contour of the body much better than paper.

GENERAL DRESSMAKING TIPS

Having gathered together all the items you need for your dressmaking project, here are a few tips to help you on your way.

✕ Prepare your paper pattern. Iron the pattern pieces – they need to lie flat on your fabric.

✕ Press your fabric, too; it will be easier to lay out your pattern and will allow for greater accuracy when cutting out. Press wool on a steam setting to pre-shrink it.

✕ Make sure your pattern is laid out following the grain line (see page 38). Follow the pattern layout for your fabric width and style.

✕ Use plenty of pins when pinning the pattern to the fabric – put pins in each corner and several along the edges (photo 1, opposite). But make sure that they don't project over the cutting line, as this will damage your scissors.

✕ Use tailor's tacks to mark where zips are to be positioned and darts are to be sewn, along with other necessary reference points on the garment (see page 37). Clues to aid construction are good!

✕ It can be difficult to identify the wrong and right sides of plain fabric, so put chalk marks on the wrong side.

✕ If in doubt about whether your fabric has a nap, pin all all pattern pieces so that they are lying in the same direction (see page 39).

✕ Cut out the individual pieces of fabric for your garment with care, using sharp scissors and following the line of the pattern pieces as accurately as possible.

✕ Remember to cut notches outwards so that they don't steal your seam allowance (see page 38).

✕ If you are right-handed, place your left hand on your pattern piece to hold it flat while cutting out (photo 2, opposite) . This will be the other way round if you are left-handed.

✕ Take care when cutting two garment pieces out of a single rather than a double layer of fabric. Cut one piece with the paper pattern print right side up, then turn the paper pattern over to cut out the second piece. You will then have a right and a left piece!

✕ Practise your machine stitching on a double piece of fabric before you make a start on your garment.

✕ Place garment pieces right sides together before you attach them, carefully matching the notches together on each seam.

✕ When you're pinning seams together, always pin at right-angles to the fitting line. This makes them easier to pull out when you're sewing the seam.

✕ As you construct your garment, remove pattern pieces one at a time, matching to the adjacent piece. This avoids confusion when you have lots of pieces. Where there are many sections of the garment to cut out, it may be helpful to label each one with a slip of paper attached with a pin so that you can identify which section it is once you have removed the paper pattern.

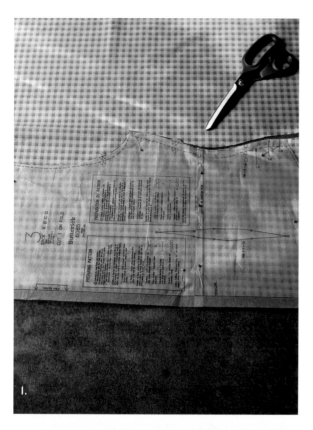

✕ Don't screw up your garment in between sewing sessions. Lay it over a hanger so that it is kept flat for the next stage.

✕ Press every seam as you make it, to bed the stitches in, and then press the seam open or to one side if that is indicated in the pattern.

✕ Neaten each seam as you construct it (see page 82). The minute you trap one seam in another with a row of machining, it is very difficult to get at it to neaten any raw edges.

✕ Trim, clip (see page 84) and press at every stage of your project.

✕ Measure, measure, measure! Be as accurate as possible when you sew. I sew with a tape measure on a lanyard around my neck!

Top Tip

Measure twice, cut once!

HAND STITCHES

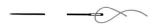

Here I've listed all the basic hand stitches that you'll need for the various projects in this book.

Overstitch or oversewing stitch: This is a small, even diagonal stitch that can be worked from either the right or the wrong side of a garment or other item being sewn together. The stitches will usually show, but give a very secure join.

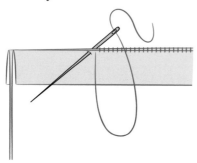

Overcast stitch: This stitch is used to neaten edges. Take a diagonal stitch over the edge of the fabric.

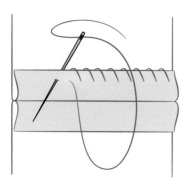

Running stitch: I often use this as a tacking or temporary stitch. It is secure and several stitches are worked at the same time.

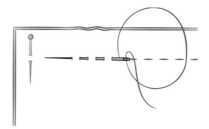

Backstitch: This is a really robust hand stitch that can be used to make permanent seams.

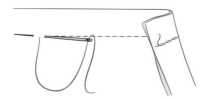

Catch stitch: I have used this to catch the side hems on my curtains (see page 190). Don't pull too tight or it will show through on the right side of the fabric.

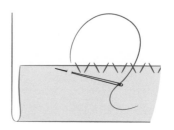

Slip stitch: This is another stitch that's used in hemming, for attaching a double fold of fabric to a single layer.

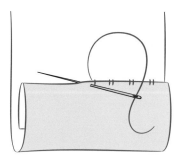

Blanket stitch: This can be used as a decorative finish for the edges of seams or appliqué motifs. The thread is looped around the needle each time it is inserted.

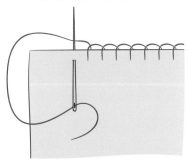

Even slip stitch (ladder stitch): I use this for catching two folds together. When pulled apart, the stitches look like the rungs on a ladder.

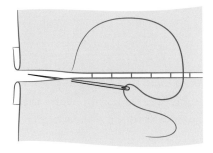

Diagonal tacking: This is really useful for holding pleats in position. When underlining a garment piece (i.e. attaching lining to the wrong side of the main fabric to help support it), as I've done in the Boned Bodice (see page 240), diagonal tacks help to hold the layers together.

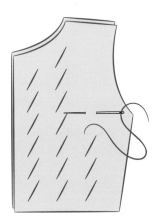

EQUIPMENT

EQUIPMENT

1. Tension regulating dial
2. Spool pin
3. Bobbin winder spindle
4. Speed control slider
5. LCD screen
6. These buttons select stitches and adjust width and length.
7. Stitch selection library and their numbers
8. Needle threader
9. Presser foot
10. Throat (needle) plate – it has markings to help guide your fabric while stitching
11. Reverse sewing button
12. One-step buttonhole foot
13. Buttonhole lever – pull down while making buttonholes

SMD 3000

JANOME

Sewing Machine

A sewing machine is an essential piece of equipment for most projects. Ideally, you want one with three controls – stitch width, stitch length and stitch selector – to give enough flexibility. There is a huge range to choose from and it's best to do a bit of research before you buy, rather than plumping for a cheap model from a catalogue or supermarket, which may be low spec and unreliable. I'd recommend visiting your nearest sewing-machine shop, where they will be able to give you a demonstration and advice on the different models so that you can select the best one for your needs. They will also provide back-up should you require it. Alternatively, is there one in the family that you can use? If it hasn't been used for a while, clean and oil it or have it serviced before you start sewing.

SEWING-MACHINE FEET

A sewing machine comes with a couple of basic 'feet' which you can use to do lots of different processes. However, more specialised feet are available that you may want to consider investing in – or putting on your wish list! – as your skills develop. Using specific feet for certain techniques can improve the quality and accuracy of your stitching.

STANDARD MACHINE FEET

Standard foot: This is the foot that you'll use for most of your sewing. The sole is fairly flat with a wide gap for working zigzag as well as running stitches.

Buttonhole foot: This either has grooves underneath for the beads of the buttonhole to go through or a plastic or metal sliding gauge.

Zipper foot: Your machine will have a standard zipper foot. These do not always stitch piping well, so you may wish to buy an adjustable one.

SPECIALISED MACHINE FEET

Here are some of my favourite machine feet and how to use them. Many different kinds are available to help with every conceivable task – I have twenty-five feet that I have collected for my machine over the years.

Invisible zipper foot: Designed specially to sew an invisible zip, as I've shown in my Shift Dress (see page 226), this has two grooves underneath to accommodate the coils of the zip while sewing in place.

Overcasting foot: This has a bar or bars and brushes to the right of the foot. The bar slackens the tension on the top thread and prevents the edge of the seam puckering up when neatening the edges of seams. If you can, use this instead of a standard foot for zigzag neatening as well as for overcasting.

Blind-stitch foot: This foot helps to guide the fabric when working a blind-stitched hem (see page 86). It can also be adjusted or positioned to aid edge stitching (see page 65).

Open embroidery foot: Ideal for appliqué or embroidery, as the wide opening at the front of the foot gives a clear view of what you are stitching, while the groove under the sole of the foot helps accommodate the denser types of stitching used in embroidery.

Walking or even-feed foot: This foot has a set of teeth on the underside that connect with the teeth on your machine, gripping both top and bottom layers of fabric when sewing and feeding them evenly through the machine. Excellent for sewing long seams on curtains or for helping to control the layers when quilting. Some models also come with a guide that fits in the back of the foot to aid parallel stitching.

Stitch-in-the-ditch foot: This foot comes with a blade in the middle of the foot. Sit this blade on the seam line and it will follow the join precisely. This foot would be perfect for guiding the stitching on the waistband of my Pencil Skirt or for the binding on the Child's Smock Apron (see pages 230 and 208).

Quarter-inch piecing foot: Position the blade of this foot over the edge of the fabric and machine. Perfect for quilting!

1. Walking foot with a quilting guide fitted on the back
2. Spare spool holder
3. Bobbins
4. Quilting guide – this fits at the back of the standard foot and aids parallel stitching
5. Buttonhole foot
6. Adjustable zipper foot
7. Standard zipper foot
8. Blind hem foot
9. Stitch in the ditch foot
10. ¼ inch seam foot
11. Overcasting foot
12. Open embroidery foot
13. Invisible zipper foot

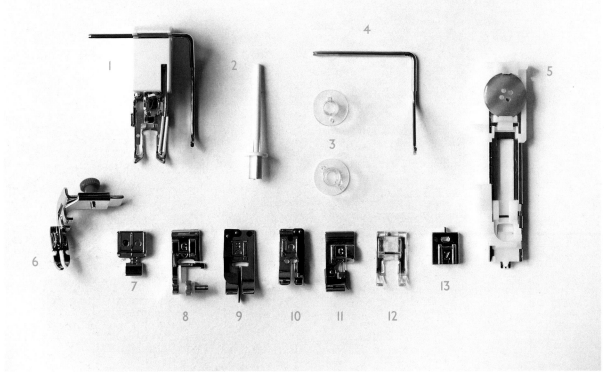

STRETCH	UNIVERSAL	TWIN NEEDLES		TOPSTITCH	UNIVERSAL	JEANS
90/14	70/9	Stretch	Stretch	80/12	80/12	90/14
		2.5/ 75	4.00/ 75	90/14		
				100/16		

 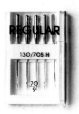     

SEWING-MACHINE NEEDLES

There are different types of machine needle for different applications – for instance, if you are sewing jersey, you wil need a ballpoint needle to avoid splitting the yarn. Once you have chosen which type, then choose a suitable size for the fabric. I've included a chart overleaf showing the different types of machine needle and their areas of application. There are many other specialist kinds of needle that you can purchase, but the ones in the list will cope with all the projects in this book.

NEEDLE SIZE

The needle 'gauge' indicates the size of the needle: the higher the number, the thicker the needle. Needles come in European and American sizing, hence the two numbers on the packet (e.g. 80/12). For the majority of your sewing projects, a universal needle size 80/12 will be fine. I have lots of different-sized needles for use in different projects. These days I tend to buy packets containing just one size rather than a mix of different sizes – it's easier to keep track of needles that way as I can no longer read the size on the shaft of the needle! Even if your eyesight is super-sharp, it's still worth putting a sticker on your sewing machine giving the size of machine needle you are currently using.

Change your needle at the end of every major project. Machine needles gradually lose their sharpness with continued use.

Don't put used needles in the same packet as new ones.

With any project it is essential to test stitch and check the needle size on a double-folded piece of the fabric.

NEEDLE TYPES & USES

Needle Type

Universal

Jersey

Stretch

Jeans

Quilting

Topstitching

Description	Area of Application	Fabrics	Needle Gauge
Standard point	Almost all natural and synthetic fabrics	Chiffon, georgette, organdie	60/8, 70/10
		Batiste/cambric, artificial silk,	70/10
		Linen, corsetry fabrics, poplin	70/10, 80/12
		Cambric, linen, suiting, velvet,	80/12, 90/14
		Heavy cotton, linen, coat fabrics	90/14, 100/16
Ballpoint for avoiding cutting knitted loops	Knitted fabrics	Jersey	70/10—100/16
Slightly rounded	Highly elastic fabrics with two-way stretch	Lycra, spandex	75/11–90/14
		Plastic foil, oilcloth	90/14
Very slim strong sharp point	Tough fabrics, artificial leather	Bedlinen, artificial leather, canvas	90/14, 100/16
		Corduroy, denim, twill	90/14–110/18
		Heavyweight fabric for working clothes	100/16, 110/18
Slim point	Suitable for quilting and sewing through multiple layers		75/11–90/14
Extra-sharp point and longer eye to accommodate thicker thread	Top and edge stitching with heavier or decorative thread		70–100

BOBBINS

The bobbin is the spool of thread inserted in the base of your machine that provides the lower thread for machine stitching. You'll need to read your machine manual for correct winding and insertion of the bobbin, but here are a few additional tips:

✕ Use the correct bobbin for your make and model of machine.

✕ Use the same thread for both bobbin and top thread to create balance when stitching. A different type of thread on the bobbin can result in uneven stitches. (There are occasions when this rule does not apply – for example, when an uneven effect is required in machine embroidery.)

✕ It's best to wind a couple of bobbins before starting a big project so that you can avoid having to stop and wind a bobbin while in the middle of sewing.

TENSION

One of my students recently referred to dealing with and understanding tension as the 'dark arts'! I thought this was really amusing as it can seem a mysterious business and any problems annoyingly hard to identify. Here's a brief explanation of how tension works in a sewing machine and what to do if things go wrong.

HOW TENSION IS CONTROLLED

Imagine that your top thread and your lower, bobbin thread are on either side of a tug-of-war team. For the perfect tension, you need your threads to be balanced and held, or 'tugged', evenly through the tension paths on the top and the bottom of your machine. The stitch should appear the same on both sides of the fabric, neither too tight nor too loose.

Upper thread tension

The thread is taken through tension discs on the upper part of your machine. When the machine foot is up, there is no tension on the thread. Put the foot down and the tension discs hold on and control the upper thread. If you have a tension dial on your machine, the middle three numbers will have a line against them, the middle number indicating the optimum level of tension.

Alternatively, your machine may give a digital readout of 0–10, in which 0 indicates no tension and 10 the maximum level. Increase the number and the tension discs will hold on more tightly. Decrease the number and the thread will be held more loosely.

Lower thread tension

Refer to the trouble-shooting section (opposite) before attempting an adjustment to bobbin tension. The tension is controlled by a tiny screw on the bobbin case and I strongly recommend you seek guidance before altering it.

Balancing tension

If the top thread is too tight or the bottom thread too loose, the bottom thread will show on the top of the seam.

If the top tension is too loose or the bottom tension is too tight, the upper thread will show on the underside of the seam.

TROUBLESHOOTING

If you are not sure what is happening to your stitching, thread the top and bottom of your machine with exactly the same type of thread but in contrasting colours and you will be able to see the stitch clearly and have a better idea of how to adjust it. Before you start altering the settings, however, check the following:

✕ Make sure your upper and lower threading is correct – refer to your sewing machine manual for advice.

✕ Is the needle damaged? You may need to replace it.

✕ Are there any fibres or bits of thread caught in the tension disc? Fold a piece of fabric in half and insert it in the tension discs and move up and down.

✕ Do the top and bobbin threads come from the same reel? Ideally, both threads should be from the same reel to ensure that the tension is evenly balanced.

✕ The screw that controls the bottom tension may vibrate loose while working on some machines. The tension can be tightened by turning the screw on the bobbin case in a clockwise direction.

MACHINE STITCHES

STRAIGHT STITCH & ZIGZAG STITCH

The two main types of machine stitch are straight or running stitch and zigzag stitch. A dial or button on your machine regulates the length of the straight stitches; the higher the number the larger the stitch. Most stitching should be sewn in the middle of the range. Another dial or button adjusts the width of the zigzag stitches; again, the higher the number the greater the width of the stitch.

If you choose a straight-stitch setting, the stitch-width dial or button for zigzag stitching can move your needle over, enabling you to work rows of stitching in different positions. With these two ways of setting stitches on your machine, you can change the length and width of any stitch.

APPLICATION OF STRAIGHT STITCH

A medium-size straight stitch is an essential for most construction techniques and decorative topstitching.

Staystitching

This is a row of machine stitching sewn inside the seam line to prevent stretching. It is usually worked on curves to support the grain – for example, along the edge of a neckline. It is worked on a single layer of fabric as soon as the paper pattern is removed.

Understitching

A row of straight machine stitching worked on the right side of the fabric close to the seam line on the facing edge of a garment. The seam allowance is trimmed, layered and clipped and then pressed to the side where the understitching will be sewn. It helps the facing to lie flat on the inside of the garment (see pages 94–97).

Topstitching

Worked on the right side of the garment using a slightly longer machine stitch, this can be decorative or functional. It can be worked with double strands of ordinary thread or thicker thread. When using double thread, either put cotton reels on two spool pins or, if your machine has only one spool pin, put two bobbins (one on top of the other) on one pin!

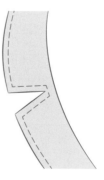

Edge stitching

A row of machine stitching worked very close to the finished edge. It can be used on pockets, pleats, collars and lapels as well as on the folded edge of a flat fell seam (see page 83).

APPLICATION OF ZIGZAG STITCH

Basic zigzag stitch in varying widths is invaluable for neatening the edge of seams or for fashioning the edges of buttonholes (see page 69). Here are a couple of useful variations.

Bar tack

This is used for reinforcement or extra strength on the top or bottom corners of pockets. Work with a medium-width zigzag stitch set with a short stitch length. Use an open embroidery foot if you are working the stitches very close together; otherwise, use an ordinary sewing-machine foot. You can also use a bar tack to make a new bar when shortening a zip (see page 113).

Three-step zigzag

I use this stitch to sew on elastic (see page 250) and to neaten the edge of a seam. For many years I did not have this stitch on my machine and I used ordinary zigzag stitch instead.

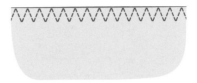

STRETCH STITCHES

Some sewing machines can produce a variety of overlock-type stitches suitable for using on cotton jersey and other knitted fabrics. You'll need an overcasting foot for working these stitches (see page 56). Vari-lock (diagram a) is primarily for fine synthetic, silk and cotton jerseys fabrics and is particularly suitable for overlocking seams and hems on pyjamas, T-shirts, sweat shirts and sportswear. Double overlock (diagram b) is suitable for all types of hand- or machine-knitted fabrics. Stretch overlock (diagram c) is good for medium-weight knits, towelling and firm wovens; use it to overlock seams and to flat join seams.

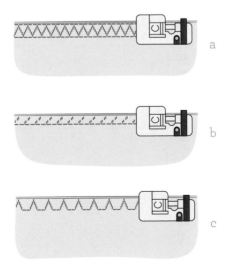

a

b

c

"Do your machine ends get in a tangle?

DOES YOUR NEEDLE UNTHREAD ITSELF?

Sew on and off

A SMALL SQUARE OF

double scrap fabric

to prevent this FROM HAPPENING."

Designed for
KNIT FABRICS ONL
Use stretchable
unbonded knits

A

B

B

A

TIPS FOR SEWING SEAMS

GUIDING YOUR MACHINE STITCHING

It is really difficult to sew in a straight line if you do not have somewhere to focus on. I was watching one of my students machining recently – the stitching line was all over the place. I asked her where she was looking while she was sewing and she said that she didn't know! Sewing in a straight line is not done by magic! You need to look at a guide on the base of the machine. Here are a few tips:

Positioning the machine needle and foot

✕ Place the machine foot so that the edge of the foot is on the edge of the fabric. Move the needle either to left or right until it is in the correct position to sew.

✕ To sew a 1.5cm (⅝in) seam, move your needle to the left until it is in the correct position.

✕ To sew edge stitching (page 65), move your needle to the right until it is just inside the edge of your fabric.

Guide bars

Consisting of a piece of metal with an angle at the end, this fits in a little hole in the back of your foot. It will move in and out and can rest on an edge of your fabric to help keep you moving in a straight line. The extension can also rest on a row of machining to enable you to work a second row of stitches parallel to the first. Great for quilting.

Guide lines

✕ Use the lines on the throat plate of your machine if they are marked. If you position the edge of your fabric correctly in relation to these lines, this will help you.

✕ A strip of coloured tape or masking tape can be applied to the base of the machine and in any position. Rest the cut or folded (if you are machining a hem) edge of your fabric beside the tape and it will act as a guide, keeping you straight.

✕ Quilter's 6mm (¼in) tape is perfect for placing along the surface of your fabric to guide your machine stitching.

✕ I have recently discovered some really fine retractable chalk pencils – draw a guide line on the fabric and machine along it.

STARTING & FINISHING A ROW OF MACHINING

Sewing machines have a reverse button and it is possible to use this button to work a few stitches at the beginning and end of a row of stitches to secure the stitching at either end. A word of warning, though! The reverse stitching works only if it is machined exactly over the row of stitching just sewn. A few stitches sewn at a jaunty angle are no good at all. They will affect the seam and make it poke out on the right side of the garment. Machine threads at either end of the seam can be threaded through the eye of a needle and a few hand stitches will secure them invisibly. Do not reverse when joining fine fabrics together, as the edge of the seam is likely to pucker.

SEWING AROUND CURVES & CORNERS

When you're sewing a curve, machine slowly and reduce the stitch length. This will give you more control. A corner needs to be sewn with a continuous row of stitching, with the stitch length reduced to strengthen the seam on either side.

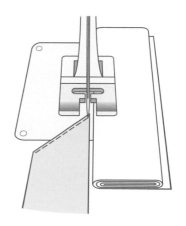

✕ Machine along the seam to within 5cm (2in) of the corner.

✕ Reduce the size of the straight stitches by adjusting the dial or pressing the button on your machine.

✕ Continue slowly machining towards the corner (which should be marked by a tailor's tack or a chalk mark) and stop.

✕ Insert the needle down at the corner, then lift the foot and turn the seam through 90 degrees. Continue machining for 5cm (2in) and adjust the stitch size back to the normal length you've been using for sewing.

SEWING THICK LAYERS

The machine can only feed the fabric if the foot is level. When stitching bulky or thick layers, place folded fabric or layers of card behind the needle and under the foot to keep the foot level. I always keep a stack of business cards in my workbox and add as many as necessary to ensure the foot remains level. Always stitch slowly.

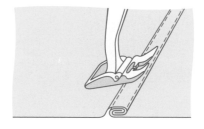

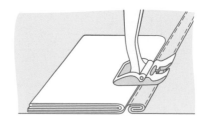

Top Tip

While stitching round a corner, particularly a sharply angled one such as the point of a collar, there is a tendency for the fabric to be pulled down the slot in the throat plate. To prevent this happening, fold a piece of fabric and position it beside the corner. It will support the machine foot and prevent pulling.

BUTTONHOLES

Buttons provide the finishing touch to a dressmaking or soft-furnishing project and so it's useful to get the hang of sewing buttonholes on your machine. As a rule, a buttonhole should be 3mm (⅛in) bigger than the button. In addition, the section of the fabric where the buttonhole is to be worked needs to be supported by a facing and possibly some interfacing.

PREPARING TO SEW

✕ Mark the position of the buttonhole with a row of tacking or a chalk pencil line from a retractable chalk pencil.

✕ Adjust the tension on your sewing machine. Loosen the top tension by setting to a lower number on your dial or read-out (see page 62). This will allow a rounder stitch to form on the right side of the buttonhole.

✕ Practise your buttonhole on layers of fabric mimicking the layers on the garment.

SEWING A BUTTONHOLE

Depending on the model of sewing machine, a buttonhole may be worked in several ways. Look at your manual to see how your particular machine makes a buttonhole and follow the instructions there. Here are a couple of tips to bear in mind when you're making one- or four-step buttonholes.

One-step buttonhole

These are created once the special foot (see page 56) has the back extended and the button has been inserted. My students often forget that there is a lever behind the foot that needs to be pulled down to engage with the foot (see photo on page 55). If this lever is not engaged, the machine will have no reference to the length of buttonhole required and will not work.

Four-step buttonhole

Attach the buttonhole foot and dial through the four stages of the buttonhole. When you've finished one buttonhole, it's important to click the dial off and click on again before making the next buttonhole. The machine will not know that you are about to start a new buttonhole if you do not do this!

CUTTING THE BUTTONHOLE

Cut the buttonhole using either a small chisel or a stitch unpicker or seam ripper. When using the latter, you need to put a pin in either end of the buttonhole to stop the unpicker or ripper accidentally cutting into the edge of the garment. When I was in the sixth form at school, I made a raincoat to take on a biology field trip. The night before the trip, I made the buttonholes. I forgot to put pins in the ends of the buttonholes and cut through them with my seam ripper straight to the front edge of the coat. Once you have done this, you never forget to use pins again! The raincoat ended up with fancy tab fastenings instead of buttons.

TWIN NEEDLES

You can use a twin needle in any machine with a wide slot in the throat plate to accommodate swing-needle or zigzag stitching. Two or more needles are attached to a single shank and inserted into the same socket as you would a single needle. For two needles you will of course need two reels of thread. If you have a second spool pin in your accessories box, you can insert it into your machine. If you don't have one, just put two bobbins one above the other on the single spool pin.

TWIN-NEEDLE SIGN

When you use twin needles, you just need to remember that they can't swing out as far as a single needle, especially if you're doing zigzag or decorative stitching. It's therefore important to engage the twin-needle sign if you have one on your machine. This prevents the needles from swinging too far out and breaking. Alternatively, set the width of your zigzag stitch to half the usual setting.

NEEDLE SIZE

You'll see two numbers on the packet for twin needles – one is the space between each needle and the other the size of the needle. For instance, 3/90 indicates there are 3mm (⅛in) of space between the needles, which are size 90 (like a standard needle). You can also buy 'stretch' needles specifically designed to work on knitted fabrics like jersey.

SEWING WITH TWIN NEEDLES

Topstitching

Twin needles create wonderful topstitching on clothing and craft work, as two perfectly parallel rows of stitching are worked at the same time.

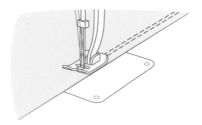

Pin-tucking a piece of fabric

Twin needles are tailor-made for creating pin tucks on fabric. Having worked a piece of fabric in this way, you can then either make it into a panel for a cushion or cut it out as section to incorporate in a garment.

1. Cut a square of fabric larger than the finished section you intend to use for a cushion or garment, as pin-tucking will make the fabric contract a little in size. Fold the fabric in half and crease.

2. Work the first tuck along the crease line.

3. Position the machine foot against the first tuck and use that as a guide to work a second tuck. Continue in this way until the piece of fabric has the number of tucks required.

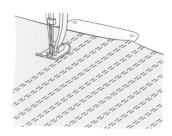

4. Rows of decorative machine stitching can be worked in between the tucks.

Shortening a T-shirt

Turn under the hem by 3cm (1¼in) and then work a row of twin-needle stitching on the right side of the garment. Trim away any surplus hem back to the line of stitching.

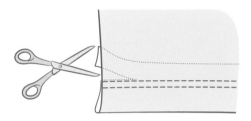

Stitching a seam on a jersey garment

Using twin needles is a good way to join seams on cotton jersey.

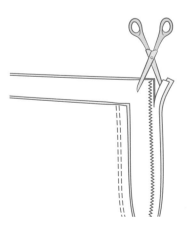

Storage: Keep your sewing machine in a warm, well-ventilated room – not in your loft or garage!

Maintenance: Keep your machine in good working order. Brush out any loose threads or bits of fluff after each major project and oil machine parts as required.

Feet: Use the correct machine foot for the stitch or technique, as this will produce a better finish.

Needle threader: Does your machine have one of these? It will only work if your needle is in its highest position and in the centre setting.

Needle: Change the needle after each large piece of work. It does not have to be broken to need changing and can become blunt with use.

Setting: Return to normal settings at the end of each task. Computerised machines will automatically return to normal settings when the machine is switched off.

Tension: When your stitching is less than perfect, first re-thread the machine before adjusting anything else on the machine.

EQUIPMENT

TROUBLESHOOTING

Below is list of common sewing-machine problems that you may encounter, along with likely causes for each problem:

Upper thread breaking

X Top thread is too tight.

X Needle inserted wrongly.

X Needle is blunt or bent.

Bottom thread breaking

X Bottom thread is too tight.

X Bobbin is jammed in its case.

X Needle hole in the throat plate is damaged.

Uneven stitch length or faulty stitches

X Wrong needle for the type of machine.

X Needle is crooked, inserted incorrectly or blunt.

X Poor-quality needle.

Needle breaks

X Needle clamp screw is not sufficiently tightened.

X The fabric has been pulled out of the machine too sharply and the needle has become bent.

X Heavy or thick layers of material have caused undue strain on the needle.

X Cheap thread has been used, which is often irregular and with occasional knots.

Puckered fabric

X Blunt or too large needle.

X The fabric is being pulled through the feed.

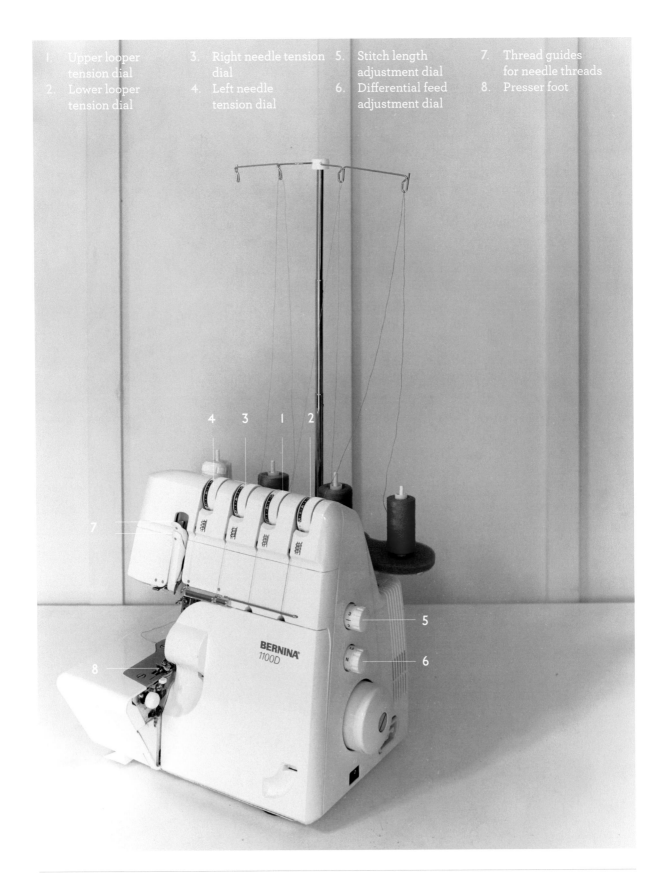

1. Upper looper tension dial
2. Lower looper tension dial
3. Right needle tension dial
4. Left needle tension dial
5. Stitch length adjustment dial
6. Differential feed adjustment dial
7. Thread guides for needle threads
8. Presser foot

Overlocker

An overlocker is designed for joining seams and neatening edges using the looped type of stitching that you see on commercially made garments. It consists of an upper and lower blade that act like a pair of scissors, trimming the fabric while the threads oversew or overlock the edges of the seam. It is this feature that makes it ideal for neatening seams. An overlocker is not an essential piece of equipment and needs to be used in conjunction with an ordinary sewing machine – you can't do a basic running stitch on one, for instance – but it is extremely useful, none the less, for creating a professional-looking finish to your garment.

FOUR-THREAD & THREE-THREAD STITCHING

The standard overlocker uses four threads: two needle threads and an upper and lower looper thread. The needle threads create the straight stitching, while the looper threads enclose or overlock the seam edges. A four-thread stitch (below left) is the most stable and is used for constructing seams, while a three-thread stitch (below right), in which the left-hand needle is removed, can be used for neatening raw edges.

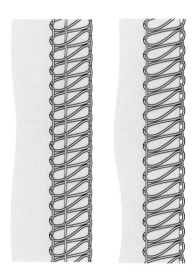

A couple of basic tips to bear in mind:

✕ When you've removed the left-hand needle for three-thread stitching, it's important to tighten the screw that held it in position so the right-hand needle doesn't wander.

✕ When you're sewing with both needles, you'll notice that the left-hand needle is higher than the right-hand one. This is intentional and doesn't need to be adjusted. I taught a course recently where a student spent rather a long time trying to make the needles level!

THREADING AN OVERLOCKER

Many a day can be spent re-threading an overlocker, so I've given a few tips here for threading and re-threading that I hope will help reduce the time spent in sheer frustration trying to get your machine to behave!

Before you start, make sure that the pressure foot on your overlocker is raised so that the threads can pass through the tension discs without getting stuck.

When you first thread your machine, use a different colour for each spool and match the colours to those on your threading guides on the front of the machine. You will then be able to see which thread goes where.

Always thread in the correct order: upper looper, lower looper, right needle, left needle. Getting the sequence right each time is vital!

RE-THREADING AN OVERLOCKER

✕ Raise the pressure foot to disengage the tension.

✕ Cut the threads above the reels.

✕ Put new reels on the spool pins and knot the new threads on to the threads on the machine.

✕ Pull the new threads through one by one, working in the correct order: upper looper, lower looper, right needle, left needle.

✕ The needle threads will need to have the knots cut off so that they can be threaded with tweezers supplied with the machine.

THREAD BREAKS WHILE SEWING

✕ First raise the pressure foot.

✕ Raise the needles and always pull the thread out of the needles and position out of the way. If you do not do this, the threads will be in the wrong sequence when you have finished threading the loopers.

✕ If the lower looper is unthreaded, re-thread and then re-thread needles.

✕ If the upper looper is unthreaded, unthread the lower looper, then re-thread upper looper, lower looper and needle threads.

✕ When re-threading, make sure that the thread is pulled into the tension discs. Sometimes it just lies on the surface and is therefore not controlled.

TENSION

As with a sewing machine, the higher the number on your tension disc, the more tightly the thread will be held in position. The optimum level of tension will vary slightly from machine to machine, so if you've just bought your overlocker, it's a good idea to make a note of the tension dial setting for future reference.

BALANCED TENSION

When the tension is perfectly balanced, the upper and lower loopers should lock together on the cut edge of the fabric and the rows of straight stitching should be in a straight line. Before you begin a project, it's best to check the tension is right. Work a sample to test the stitching with the tension dials set in the middle of their range. Practise on a double layer of fabric as if you were working a seam. It can also be useful to note the tension settings when you start sewing a garment and keep a record of any settings that produced a good stitch for a particular process.

ADJUSTING THE TENSION

Don't be afraid to change the tension settings. Unlike the domestic sewing machine, overlockers need tension adjustments for different stitches. Indeed, before you re-thread your overlocker, it's always best to check the tension settings first, just in case the problem lies there. Adjust one dial at a time and do a test piece after each adjustment. Return to the same setting if no improvement is made. This will prevent you from getting too confused!

GENERAL TIPS FOR SEWING WITH AN OVERLOCKER

✕ Before you start, make a note of factory settings. Whenever you use your overlocker, record those settings that produce a good stitch.

✕ Keep your machine well maintained: brush out dust and fluff and oil regularly.

✕ Make sure the mast at the back of the overlocker is fully extended before you start to sew.

✕ Make sure all threads are moving freely and are not caught on any part of the machine.

✕ You do not need to lift the foot up completely before beginning to sew. Simply insert the fabric under the front edge of the foot and stitch to the end of the seam until a chain is worked that can then be cut.

✕ If the machine is not stitching properly after re-threading, make sure that the threads are engaged in between the tension discs.

✕ Missed stitches usually indicate a blunt needle. Rather than trying to identify which needle to change, I recommend replacing both needles to be on the safe side.

DIFFERENTIAL FEED

Most modern overlockers have a differential feed consisting of two sets of feed dogs or teeth that move fabric along as you stitch. They can be adjusted depending on what you're sewing. The two feed dogs move independently, each travelling at a different rate. This prevents fluting or waving in knitted or stretch fabrics. It also ensures pucker-free seams in smooth fabrics such as nylon or closely woven cloth.

SETTING THE DIFFERENTIAL FEED

When the differential feed is set to a higher number, the front feed will move faster than the back one. This prevents the fabric from stretching. When the differential feed is set to a lower number, the front teeth will move more slowly or in time with the back teeth. This prevents the fabric from puckering.

The higher setting enables one to create wave-free seams on heavier or very stretchy fabrics, while the lower setting helps to prevent puckering on lightweight fabrics. See the chart opposite for further detail.

DIFFERENTIAL FEED SETTINGS

Setting	How the teeth are moving	Effect on fabric	Fabric suitability
0.5–0.7	Front teeth are moving more slowly than the back teeth, holding the fabric taut	Prevents puckering on lightweight fabrics	Fine nylon jersey, closely woven fabrics, linings, satin and cotton
Normal	Both sets of teeth are moving at the same rate	Fabric feeds normally, creating an even seam	Woven fabric
1.5	Front teeth are moving slightly faster than the back teeth	Wave-free seams	Cotton, silk, synthetic jersey, sweatshirt fabric and fine knits
2–2.5	Front teeth feed faster than the back teeth, pushing fabric together	Wave-free seams	Thick wool knits, hand-knitted articles and very stretchy fabrics

TECHNIQUES

SEAMS

Seams are an essential part of the construction of a garment and they will vary according to where they are in the garment and the weight of the fabric. The width of the seam may vary, too, depending on where it is. Clothing patterns usually give a 1.5cm (⅝in) seam allowance, although on some occasions it may be less or more. It's always a good idea to check before you start sewing.

TACKING

Tacking is a form of basic hand stitch used to attach two pieces of fabric after pinning them together and before machine-stitching the join. Whether you go through the whole process of pinning, tacking and machining or just pinning and machining depends partly on the complexity of the join and partly on your own level of confidence. As with everything in sewing, though, the more thorough you are in your preparation, the better the end result will be.

Start each seam line with a couple of stitches to secure the thread. I prefer fastening thread in this way rather than using a knot, as a knot can pull through the fabric.

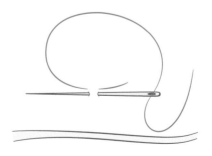

Once you've secured the end of the thread, stitch small even stitches, about 1cm (½in) wide, to attach the two pieces of fabric prior to machine-stitching. Secure the end of the seam with a couple of stitches, as you did at the start.

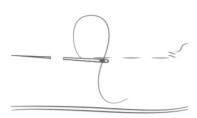

PLAIN SEAM

This is the most commonly used seam for attaching parts of a garment or other items. It can be used on most fabrics and can be opened out and pressed flat for a strong, smooth finish.

1. Pin and tack your two pieces of fabric right sides together, then machine-sew along the fitting line, using medium-sized stitches.

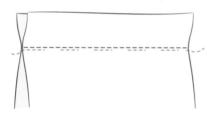

2. Press the seam open.

3. Neaten the edges with edge stitching (top seam) or narrow binding (bottom seam).

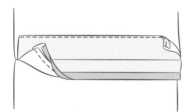

Alternatively, trim the seam allowance to 1cm (½in) and neaten with zigzag stitch (top seam) or an overcasting foot with an overcasting stitch on your sewing machine (bottom seam).

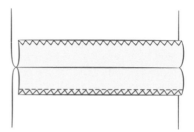

As an alternative finish for a plain seam – good for reinforcing a crotch on trousers for children – you could try the following:

1. Sew your first row of stitching, then position the machine foot against it so that the left side of the foot aligns with the stitching and work a second row of stitching parallel to it.

2. Trim to just outside this second row of stitching.

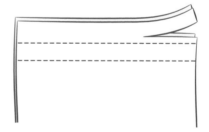

3. Zigzag the edges together and press the seam allowance to one side.

FRENCH SEAM

This is a fabulous seam for lingerie, fine garments and children's wear. It provides a really neat finish on sheer fabrics and any lightweight material that frays easily, as all raw edges are enclosed. A French seam is very strong and durable. It is not suitable for use on heavy fabrics, however, as it would create a lumpy effect along the seams of the garment.

1. Place the two pieces of fabric wrong sides together and machine 6mm (¼in) from the raw edge. Press the seam open and trim the edges to 3mm (⅛in) from the stitching.

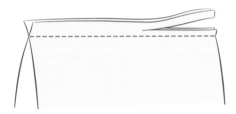

2. Turn the seam inside out so that the two pieces of fabric are now right sides together and roll the stitch line to the edge with your fingers. Stitch along the fitting line.

3. Press the seam to one side, towards the back of the garment.

FLAT FELL SEAM

This a very robust seam, suitable for use on side and shoulder seams and along armholes. It is ideal for jeans and children's clothes and gives a beautifully clean finish.

1. Place the two pieces of fabric wrong sides together and machine-stitch 1.5cm (⅝in) from the raw edge.

2. Press the seam open and then press it to one side, helping the seam line to lie flat on the inside.

3. Trim the inner raw edge to 6mm (¼in) and the outer edge to 1.3cm (½in).

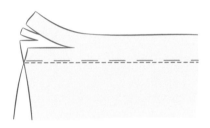

4. Fold the wider outer edge over the narrower inner edge and press under to form a 6mm (¼in) fold.

5. Pin and tack the seam flat towards the back of the garment, then machine-stitch close to the folded edge.

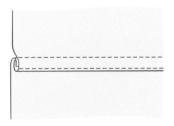

TRIMMING & CLIPPING

Seam allowances are trimmed to reduce bulk in enclosed seams such as those in collars, cuffs, front facings and shaped hems. Meanwhile, clipping helps to ease the tension in fabric along curved edges.

TRIMMING & LAYERING

If one seam joins another one, trim off the ends of the joining seam at an angle.

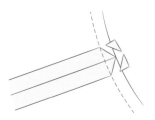

On the point of a collar, cut the seam off diagonally at the tip and layer the seam allowances.

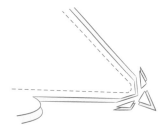

If the seam edges are 'blunt cut' (i.e. cut to the same length), it can make a ridge along the seams on the inside of the garment. To avoid this, it's a good idea to layer or grade the edges. First, trim any interfacing close to the row of machining.

Cut the next layer to 5mm (¼in) and the last layer, the one that sits next to the garment when turned through, to about 7mm (⅜in).

CLIPPING

Inwardly curving seams need to be clipped at intervals to prevent tightness. Clip with the tips of a small, very sharp pair of scissors along a concave curve such as a neckline. Again, I layer the edges wherever possible.

NOTCHING WITH PINKING SHEARS

Outwardly curving seams need to be cut, too, to reduce bulk. Although it's standard practice to cut notches at intervals along a convex seam, I personally never do this as notches are inclined to poke out at each point when you turn the fabric the right way out. To give a more even reduction of bulk and hence a smoother effect on the right side of the garment, I recommend using pinking shears instead or trimming seams closer to the stitching.

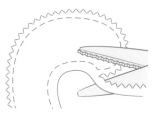

HEMS

These are the finishing touch to any garment or other sewing project and need to be handled with care.

ENSURING A HEM IS LEVEL

This is tricky to do 'solo'. It's best to enlist the help of a friend or member of the family, if you can. Dressmaking for myself over the years, I have turned up many a hem, and my husband has become an expert at measuring and pinning a line for me to follow! If you're making the garment for someone else, then it's much simpler, of course,

1. First put the garment on together with the shoes that you'll be wearing with it. This is important as the height of the heels alters the tilt of your body and hence the way the garment hangs.

2. If you can, get a friend or member of the family to stand a long ruler or rigid tape measure on the ground next to you in order to ensure the hem remains level as it's pinned. He or she should move round you putting in pins at regular intervals to mark the line of the hem.

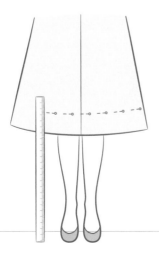

3. Remove the garment and put it over your ironing board so that you can rotate the hem to check the pinning. Ignore any pins at a jaunty angle – you probably breathed at the moment this pin was positioned!

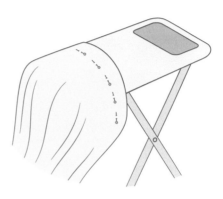

4. Take the garment off the ironing board, fold the hem up along the row of pins and tack into position.

5. Place the garment back on the ironing board, wrong side out this time. Use a sewing gauge, tape measure or ruler to help you mark the hem so that you can cut it level. While you do this, place a piece of paper beneath the folded-over edge of the fabric – this will prevent you from inadvertently cutting through to the front of the garment.

6. Choose a method for finishing the edge of the hem (see page 86).

FINISHING HEMS BY HAND

For the smoothest, least visible finish, a hand-stitched hem is best provided it's done well. You just need to remember not to pull the stitches too tight as the fabric will pucker slightly on the right side of the garment.

Blind-stitched hem

A fantastic hem for any garment or set of curtains as it is totally invisible.

1. Turn up the hem allowance and neaten the edge with zigzag or an overcasting stitch on your sewing machine (see page 65).

2. Tack around the hem 5mm (¼in) from the neatened edge and press it in place.

3. Fold the hem away from the garment along the point at which you will be stitching.

4. Secure the thread at one end of the hem, then, working from right to left, catch a couple of threads on the inside of the folded edge of the garment and take a small stitch in the hem. Continue in this way until you have completed the hem.

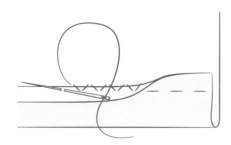

Slip hemming or slip-stitched hem

This hem is used to finish fabrics that fray easily and need to be folded over twice to enclose raw edges. It's ideal for curtains, but not appropriate for clothes made from thick fabric as a ridge will form on the right side of the garment.

1. Secure the thread at one end of the hem and slide the needle into the folded edge of the hem, bringing it out after about 1cm (½in). Pick up a couple of threads on the back of the garment or curtain and then slide the needle into the hem again.

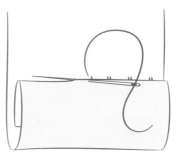

2. Continue in this way along the hem.

FINISHING HEMS BY MACHINE

Machined hems are more robust than ones sewn by hand, but you'll need to keep the stitching absolutely straight. For certain projects, such as the Express Bunting (see page 136), a decorative machine stitch (see page 88) can be an ideal way of finishing a hem. It looks wonderful as well as being very strong.

Blind-stitched hem

A blind-stitch foot (see page 56) can be purchased for most sewing machines and this really helps when positioning the fabric.

1. Turn up the hem allowance and neaten the edge with zigzag or an overcasting stitch on your sewing machine (see page 65).

2. Tack the hem into position 5mm (¼in) from the neatened edge..

3. Fold the garment along the tacked line of stitching and away from the hem so that the neatened edge of the hem appears to your right. Position the sewing machine with the machine foot to the right of the fold and adjust the stitch width or swing of the needle so that the zigzag stitch just catches the fold. This will take a few minutes to position to ensure the stitch is invisible on the right side of the garment.

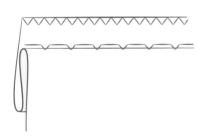

Double-turned hem

These are really strong and hence ideal for finishing children's clothes, crafts and curtain linings. They can be any size and are literally fabric that has been turned over twice and sewn. They only work well on curved edges if they are narrow.

1. Press the edge of the hem towards you to the wrong side of the fabric. I use a sewing gauge to measure the amount that I turn under.

2. Turn under again along the inside edge of the hem and machine along the inner fold.

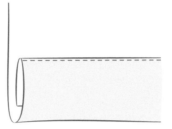

Machine-rolled hem

This is a lovely way of creating a fine rolled hem.

1. Cut out the fabric with a hem allowance of 1.5cm (⅝in) and machine-stitch 1.3cm (½in) from the raw edge.

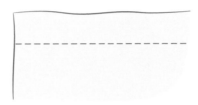

2. Fold the fabric along this row of machining and, with the wrong side uppermost, machine along the edge of the fold.

3. Trim the edge of the fabric back to this second row of machining.

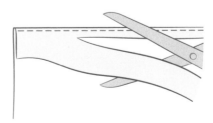

TECHNIQUES

4. Roll the hem over again along this second row of stitching and machine in place.

Pin hem

Pin hem

This is very similar to the machine-rolled hem except that the last stage is slip-stitched. It takes longer to complete but creates a beautiful hand finish. Follow steps 1–3 of the machine-rolled hem and then slip-stitch to finish (see page 51).

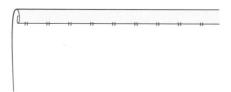

Tucked hem

These are great on children's clothes as the tuck is both decorative and creates an extra piece of fabric that can be used to lengthen the garment.

1. Turn the hem over once, then press and tack in place.

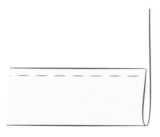

2. Fold the hem over again and tack and topstitch the edge parallel with the fold.

3. This creates a tuck on the right side of the garment. For decorative effect, you could then stitch another tuck above the first one.

Decorative hem

Use a decorative stitch on your sewing machine to secure this hem. Work from the right side of the garment for the best results.

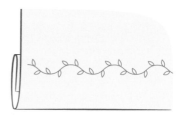

Shaped hem

This is a very useful technique for producing shaped hems, such as the scallops on the bottom of the Puppet Theatre (see page 140). Drawing shapes on fabric and cutting out after machining maintains the stability of the fabric. Sewing curves or complex shapes is easier if you first reduce the size of your machine stitch to below the average range.

1. Place your pieces of fabric right sides together and then draw the shape – ideally using a template as for the Puppet Theatre – on the wrong side of the doubled-up fabric. Machine-stitch along these lines.

2. Cut out the shaped hem, then either trim the edges to 3mm (⅛in) with medium-size scissors or using a pair of pinking shears. Clip the inner curve with the tips of a small sharp pair of scissors.

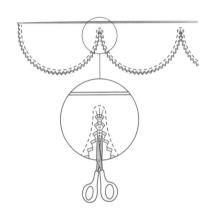

3. Turn through to the right side of the fabric and push the shape out with a point turner or chopstick to ensure the seam is right at the edge. Press to finish.

PRESSING

Press your paper pattern and your project or garment at every stage. If you wait until the garment is finished, you will have buckled trapped seams, wonky curves and much more!

There's a difference between pressing and ironing. Pressing means pressing the iron onto the fabric and lifting it straight up again. Ironing involves sliding the iron across the garment and can cause wrinkles. Press the seams as you go to bed the stitches in. Then press the seam open or to one side, as indicated in the pattern. If seam neatening distorts the edge, I press both seam and neatened edges as I sew them. Then I open them and press with a seam roll or paper underneath the seam allowance. Seam edges are more pronounced when neatened and can make a ridge on the right side of the garment.

Pressing guidelines

✕ Always test the temperature of the iron.

✕ Press on the wrong side of your garment whenever possible, to prevent shine and indentation on seam lines and details. If you must press on the right side, use a muslin pressing cloth.

✕ Never press over pins, as you will get a row of dents – not a good look!

✕ Press darts and seams before joining that piece to another part of the garment.

✕ Use steam from the iron or lay a damp piece of muslin over the area you're pressing to encourage the fabric to lie flat.

MITRING A CORNER

I have to say that I am a compulsive mitrer! It is a brilliant way to neaten a corner, such as on a napkin or a Roman blind (see pages 124 and 184). I'd advise practising on a piece of paper first to perfect your technique. The mitres I've given here are both symmetrical; for an asymmetrical mitre, ideal for use on a curtain, see page 194.

SINGLE-FOLD MITRE

This type of mitre is created in a single layer of folded-over fabric. It would be suitable where the hems meet at the top of a curtain, for instance, or where a kick pleat in a skirt meets a hem.

1. Fold over the edges of your fabric to the wrong side and press to make a crease on the outer edge. Open out the fabric again.

2. Fold over the corner at 45-degrees at the point where the two creases meet.

3. Fold in each side of the corner.

DOUBLE-FOLD MITRE

This is a really neat way to finish napkins (see page 124). It's used where you have a double layer of fabric folded over.

1. Fold over the edges of the fabric and press in place, as in step 1 of the single-fold mitre, then fold over again to create a double crease on all sides. Open out the fabric again.

2. Fold over the corner at a 45-degree angle across the inner junction of the crease lines. Trim off the point of the corner turning. (It can be easier to do this once you've created the mitre and can see how much fabric is protruding.)

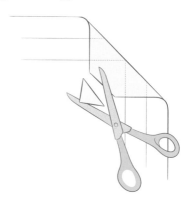

3. Turn over all the edges to the first crease, then fold over again along the second crease line. This forms a wonderful double hem with a mitred corner.

4. Working on the right side of the fabric, secure the hem with your sewing machine using topstitching or a pretty embroidery stitch (see page 84).

DARTS

Darts are a simple way to add shape to a flat piece of fabric to enable it to fit the contours of the body. They are stitched on folded fabric and are shaped to a point to mark the place where the garment flattens out again. Single-pointed darts are used to shape the bust, while double-pointed darts, positioned vertically, are used to shape the waist on a dress, such as on my Shift Dress (see page 226). For both types of dart, you will need to do the following:

1. Transfer the position of the darts with tailor's tacks (see page 42).

2. Fold the fabric right sides together, pinning the pairs of tailor's tacks exactly together. The single tailor's tack will mark the point at the end of the single-pointed dart or at each end of the double-pointed dart.

3. Lay a ruler along the line of tailor's tacks from the wide end to the point (or points) and draw a guideline with a chalk pencil.

SINGLE-POINTED DART

1. Machine from the wide end of the dart to the point in a straight line.

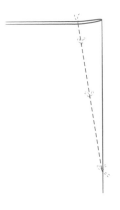

2. Remove the tailor's tacks and press the stitching with an iron.

3. Press the dart to one side.

DOUBLE-POINTED DART

1. Machine from one single tailor's tack through to the centre of the dart and then out to the second single tailor's tack.

2. Remove the tailor's tacks and press the stitching, then press the dart towards the centre of the garment.

3. This dart may need to be clipped in the middle if it is deep and might otherwise pull on the right side of the garment. You will need to neaten the clipped edge with oversewing.

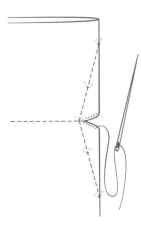

GATHERING

This is a really great way to distribute fullness evenly on skirts, frills, sleeve crowns and much more. Here, two rows of stitching are worked using the longest machine stitch, but the same effect can be achieved using small running stitches worked by hand.

1. Set your stitch length to no. 4 or the largest running stitch. Work a row of stitches on the right side of the fabric just inside the fitting line. Position your machine foot against the first row of gathering and work a second row.

2. Measure the width of the piece to be gathered and the width of the piece to which you are going to attach it. Divide both pieces into the same number of sections (say, four) and mark the start and end of each section with a pin. Place the flat piece right side up on your work surface, with the gathered piece right side down on top, matching the pin markers of each section. Pin the layers together.

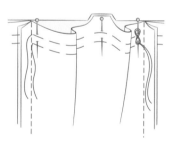

3. Wind one end of both bobbin threads on the two rows of gathering around a pin in a figure-of-eight. At the other end of the row of gathering, carefully pull up the bobbin threads until the gathered piece is the same width as the flat piece. Distribute the gathers evenly.

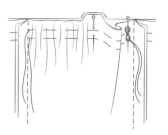

4. Pin the two layers together at right angles to hold the gathering in place. Machine the two layers together on seam line, gathered side up, just inside the lower or wider gathering thread. Don't forget to shorten your machine stitch! Work a second row of machining parallel with the first.

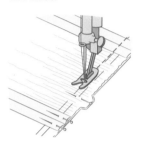

5. Remove the gathering threads. Trim the seam allowance to just outside the second row of machining and then zigzag the edges to neaten them.

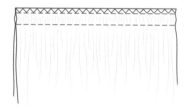

Don't be tempted to use a twin-needle - all you will get are pin tucks!

4/10

" *Take Time*

to distribute

THE GATHERS

evenly."

FACINGS

Facings are used to finish necklines, armholes, waistlines and any shaped edges. They should be invisible on all but jackets, coats or open-neck garments where there is a collar and revers. Facings are usually cut out of the same fabric as the garment, though sometimes they can be in a different fabric in a contrasting colour as a design feature for a coat or shirt.

FITTING

The facing is an exact replica in shape to the garment edge you are finishing. If you alter the shape of the garment by taking it in, letting it out or changing the shape in any other way in the area that is faced, you must make exactly the same alteration to your facing. Failure to do this will result in a poor finish. I always recommend adjusting the facing after you have altered the relevant part of the garment.

INTERFACING

A facing usually has a layer of interfacing or stiffening attached to the wrong side to give it body. When choosing an interfacing, it's best to go for one in a similar weight or lighter than the main fabric or it will give too much rigidity to the facing (see page 31). You attach the interfacing first, either ironing or tacking it onto the wrong side of the facing, then join the seams of the facing together. Neaten the outer edges either by making a small hem, zigzag stitching on the machine or overlocking.

ARMHOLE FACING

An armhole facing provides a classic way of finishing a sleeveless dress or blouse.

1. The bodice seams must be completed before you attach the facing. With right sides together, join the shoulder and underarm seams of the facing, then press open. Neaten the outer edge of the facing with a small hem.

2. Position the facing on the right side of the bodice, matching shoulder, side seams and notches.

3. Pin, tack and machine along the fitting line of the garment – usually 1.5cm (⅝in) from the raw edges.

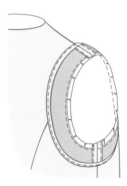

4. Trim and clip the edges (see page 84) and press the seam allowance towards the facing, then understitch (see page 64) along the facing side of the join next to the seam line.

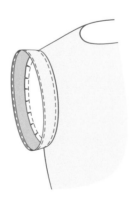

5. Press the facing to the inside of the garment and secure in position with a few hand stitches on the side and shoulder seams.

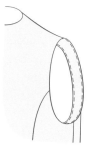

NECK FACING

Where the garment has a simple neckline with no opening, the neck facing is identical in construction to the armhole facing. If there is an opening at the neck for a fastening or zip, the facing is made in three rather than two sections, the back sections joining each of the back sections of the garment, as for the waist facing (see page 96).

COMBINED NECK & ARMHOLE FACING

Many of my students have asked me to include a combined neck and armhole facing in this book. It's a great way to finish the neckline and armholes of a garment at the same time. You could use it for a top or a dress – any garment with a seam at the back.

1. First cut out your top and facings. Pin your garment right sides together at the shoulder seams, machine together and neaten the seams.

2. Place the facings right sides together, then pin and machine-stitch the shoulder seams. Neaten the lower edge of the facings with a small hem.

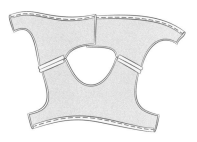

3. Position the right side of the facing on the right side of the garment and pin and tack the neck edges together. Machine into position and trim and clip the edges.

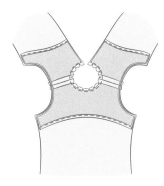

4. Press the seam allowance towards the facing and understitch (see page 64) the facing from the right side.

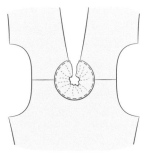

5. Press the facing to set a smooth line around the neck edge.

6. Now turn the facing inside out again so that it is right sides together with the garment. Pin, tack and machine the armholes, then trim and clip the seams.

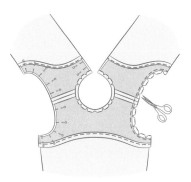

7. Now for the magic bit! Pull each back section through the 'tunnel' at each shoulder seam. It will be easier if you attach a large safety pin to the corner at the base of the side seam and use this to guide each back section through its shoulder tunnel. Press the facing at the neck and armholes.

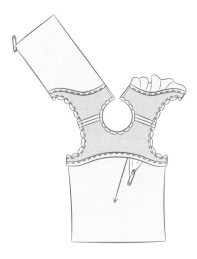

8. Put the front and back of the garment right sides together and match the side seams, particularly the underarm seam that joins the facing to the garment.

Pin and machine the side seams together, starting at the neatened edge of the facing and continuing down to the lower edge of the garment.

9. Sew the centre back seam together and insert the fastening of your choice. It is really easy to alter a garment constructed in this way as you simply lift up the facing under the arm at each side of the garment so that you can adjust the seam linking facing and garment in one manoeuvre!

WAIST FACING

This is a brilliant way to finish a waistline on a skirt. It's really comfortable to wear as the seam sits right at the waist and is less constricting than a waistband.

1. Attach the interfacing to the wrong side of each section of the facing – I have shown a tacked-in version, but you could use fusible interfacing. Place the sections right sides together and join the seams. Press the seams open and neaten the lower edge (with the longer curve). I have used a zigzag stitch on this one, but you could make a small hem, as for the previous facings.

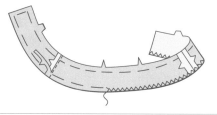

2. Pin the facing to the waistline of the skirt with right sides together and matching the notches. Pin, tack and machine in place.

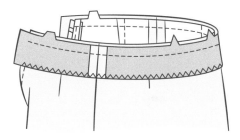

3. Now grade the seams. Not out of 10! I'm referring here to trimming the different layers of the seam edges. Trim the interfacing right back to the seam line, the facing seam a little wider, and the edge of the garment a little wider still. This reduces the bulk and has a softening effect on the trimmed turnings (see page 84).

4. Clip the waistband seam, then press the seam allowance towards the facing. Understitch (see page 64) by stitching through facing and seam allowance.

5. Turn the facing to the inside of the skirt and press in place. Catch the edges of the facing at the seams and darts, holding it in position, and slip-stitch the back openings to the openings of the skirt.

ATTACHING A COLLAR WITH A FACING

To attach a collar with a facing to a garment, you need to be really accurate at every stage. A lovely way to neaten the back neck seam of a collar is with a small piece of ready- or home-made bias binding about 2.5cm (1in) wide (see page 104). This creates a beautiful finish along the back neck seam and is really comfortable to wear. The binding should be long enough to neaten the back neck edge and a little bit extra either end to come under the facing.

PREPARING THE FRONT FACINGS

1. Make a tiny snip at the neck edge of each front facing on the line marking the position of the fold line. Make tiny snips as a guide to positioning the ends of the collar on the neck edge of the main garment piece (photo 1 on page 99) and facing. Cut out and attach interfacing (fusible or sew-in – see page 31) to each front facing, trimming the interfacing a little on the neck and outer edges of the facing to help reduce bulk in the seams later.

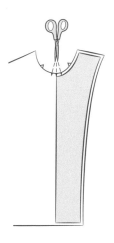

2. Neaten the outer edge of each facing with a small machined hem.

MAKING THE COLLAR

1. Mark all the balance marks (see page 38). The paper pattern will give you shoulder points on the collar, but you'll need to add a centre back marking. Mark these points with tailor's tacks (see page 42).

2. Cut out and attach a piece of interfacing to the wrong side of one of the collar pieces.

3. Place the collar pieces right sides together and mark the seam allowance on the edges – a fine chalk pencil is good for this. Leaving the neck edge open, machine stitch along the marked line.

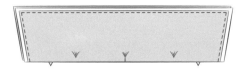

4. Trim the seam edges on the outer edge of the collar (photo 2), grading the layers (see page 84).

5. Turn the collar right side out. Use a point turner or chopstick to gently poke out all edges and then carefully roll the seam line to the edge

between a dampened forefinger and thumb. Press flat.

ATTACHING THE COLLAR & FACINGS

1. Pin and machine together the shoulder seams of the garment, press open the seams and neaten the raw edges (see page 82). Each shoulder seam should be exactly 1.5cm (⅝in); the collar will not fit if you go freestyle on these seams!

2. Carefully match the following points: the centre back of the collar to the centre back of the garment; the shoulder seam tailor's tacks on the collar to the shoulder seams on the garment; the edges of the collar to the centre front snips on the garment.

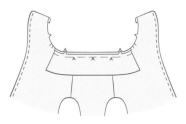

3. Pin in between all these points and tack the collar into position (photo 3), with a seam allowance of exactly 1.5cm (⅝in). Measure each end of the collar and check that they are the same length.

4. Fold back each front facing along the snip you made to mark the fold line. Match notches, sandwiching the collar.

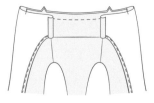

5. Fold under the shoulder seam edge of each facing.

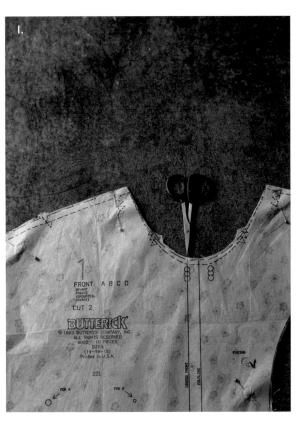

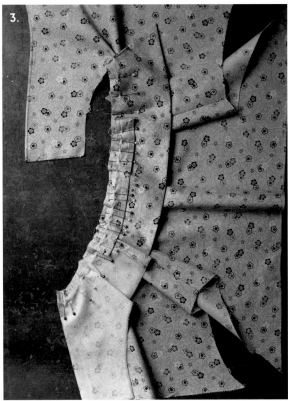

SET-IN SLEEVES

Set-in sleeves can be tricky to insert as the curved edge at the top of the sleeve (known as the crown) is fuller or has a greater circumference than the upper part of the armhole. The crown will need to be eased into position so that it fits the armhole.

1. Position the right side of the bias binding so that the first fold sits on the fitting line along the neck edge. It needs to come just beyond the folded edge of the front facing at each end.

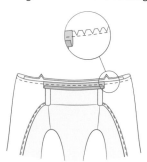

2. Machine from the folded edge of one front facing, along the neck edge, incorporating the binding, to the end of the other facing.

3. Layer the seam edges to reduce bulk and clip the curve around the neck edge.

4. Turn the front facings right sides out, using the point turner or chopstick to push out the seams and edges, and press in place.

5. Fold the bias binding in half so that it wraps around the neck seam and hand-sew the second fold of the binding into the machine stitching on the neck edge.

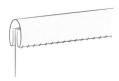

6. Catch the shoulder seam edge of each front facing to the shoulder seams of the garment with a few hand stitches.

1. At the top of the sleeve, on the right side of the fabric, work a row of ease or gathering stitches along the seam line using a large machine stitch. Put your machine foot against the first row, with the stitching to the left of the foot, and work a second row within the seam allowance.

2. With right sides together, pin, tack and machine the sleeve seam. Neaten the seam (see page 82) and press open. Repeat for the second sleeve.

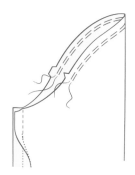

3. With right sides together, pin, tack and machine the shoulder and side seams of the garment. Neaten the seams and press open.

4. Insert the sleeve into the armhole, with right sides together, and pin together, putting your pins into the sleeve itself so that you can see the fullness at all times.

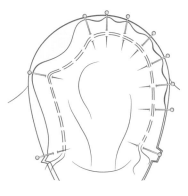

Now comes the important bit! Make sure that you match up the following marker points to help you to fit the sleeve into the armhole:

✕ Pin the underarm seams of sleeve and garment together first.

✕ Match the notches in the armhole and sleeve – single at the front and double at the back.

✕ Match the tailor's tack marking the centre of the sleeve crown to the shoulder seam.

✕ Match tailor's tacks in the sleeve marking where the easing starts to points marked with tailor's tacks on the armhole.

5. Once you have pinned the sleeve into position, gently pull up the ease stitches. The bobbin thread always pulls up more easily, which is why you machined your ease stitches on the right side of the sleeve so that the bobbin stitches would be facing you when you put in the sleeve.

6. Distribute the gathers evenly across the top of the sleeve and pin in place, then tack the sleeve into position using small stitches. Turn right side out and check before machining.

7. Starting at the underarm seam on the sleeve side of armhole, slowly machine the sleeve into the armhole (diagram 65), using your fingers to gently control the fullness of the sleeve at the crown. Overlap the stitching when you reach the starting point.

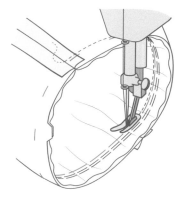

8. Remove the tacking.

9. Put your machine foot against the first row of machining and work a second row on the seam side of the armhole.

10. Trim back to just outside this second row of machining and zigzag the raw edges. The seam round the armhole of the garment should project into the sleeve rather than towards the body. This helps to give the sleeve crown a rounded appearance.

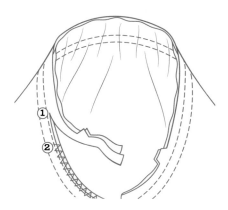

CASINGS

Casings are a good way of making a channel for cord or elastic – to hold up a pair of trousers, for instance. Choose non-twist elastic as it will stay flat once inserted. The width of the casing depends on the width of the elastic to be threaded through. If the elastic is 2.5cm (1in) wide, for example, you will need a casing 3cm (1¼in) wide to allow for movement of the elastic within the casing.

1. At the edge of the garment, fold the fabric over by 1cm (½in) to the wrong side of the garment and press, then fold over by 3cm (1¼in) and press again.

2. Edge-stitch along the top folded edge of the casing and along the bottom folded edge, leaving a 5cm (2in) gap.

3. Measure the length of elastic required. For a waist casing, you will need the waist measurement plus 6cm (2½in) for an overlap of 3cm (1¼in) at each end of the elastic.

4. Pin one end of the elastic to the garment, then thread the elastic through the casing, using a safety pin or a bodkin to pull the elastic through (diagram a). Overlap the ends of the elastic by 3cm (1¼in) and stitch together securely with the sewing machine (diagram b).

a   b

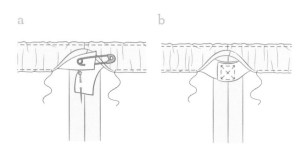

ATTACHING FLAT ELASTIC

This method of attaching elastic is really useful for lingerie or nightwear as well as for craft projects. I've included two methods here, one for attaching narrow elastic, such as on the edge of sleeves, and the other wide elastic, such as on a waistband. When you are attaching elastic in a circle, it's best to use the free arm on your machine as this is purpose built for sewing tubular items like sleeves and trouser legs.

NARROW ELASTIC

For many years I used standard zigzag stitch for this as my sewing machine had only a limited stitch selection. Most machines these days have a three-step zigzag stitch, which is ideal for this purpose.

1. Cut the elastic to the required length, allowing a seam for joining.

2. Divide the elastic into sections, to match the seams on the garment, marking each section with a pin. For a waist slip, for instance, you'd mark the centre back, centre front and side seams on the elastic.

3. Start by securing the first end of the elastic on the wrong side of the garment. Stretch the first section of elastic over to the first seam and stitch in place using three-step zigzag.

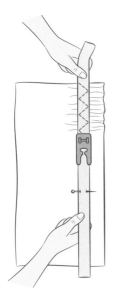

4. Repeat with the other sections; the fullness of the garment will be evenly distributed this way.

WIDE ELASTIC

1. As for narrow elastic, cut the elastic to the required length, allowing a seam for joining.

2. Divide the elastic up into sections, as for narrow elastic, then stretch the first section of elastic over to the first seam and attach using several rows of parallel straight stitching, each 5mm (¼in) apart.

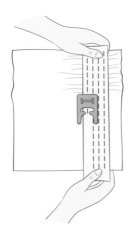

3. Repeat with the other sections.

DOUBLE FRILL

This technique is a useful one to bear in mind for giving a decorative finish to the edge of a skirt or cushion.

1. Cut out two strips of fabric – one needs to be at least 2.5cm (1in) wider than the other. Here the first strip is 6cm (2½in) wide and the second strip 10cm (4in) wide.

2. Place both strips right sides together and machine them 1cm (½in) from the raw edge.

3. Open out the lower and upper pieces of frill and make a 1cm (½in) tuck in the upper piece.

4. Fold under the lower piece to create a tuck below the first one, bringing the raw edge up behind to align with the raw edge of the upper frill. Press into position.

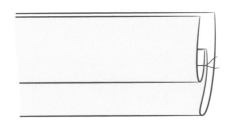

MAKING BINDING

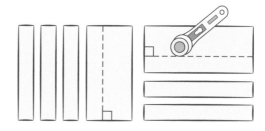

You can buy binding ready made, but to have binding in the same fabric as the item you're making, or in a colour that's not available ready made, you'll need to make your own. Either way, home-made binding means that you have a much broader choice. Unless you're making binding that you simply fold in half (as for a patchwork quilt – see page 106), you'll need a bias binding and tape maker for folding over both edges of the binding (see opposite), but these are easy to use and inexpensive to buy.

CUTTING & JOINING STRIPS OF FABRIC

When making straight binding for ties, for instance, or for attaching bunting triangles (see page 136), the fabric can be cut on the straight grain of the fabric. When binding round curves or covering piping, the strips need to be cut on the bias – in other words, cut diagonally across the fabric rather than in a straight line following the grain. This creates enough 'give' in the binding for it to curve around edges. Here are some basic instructions for cutting out and joining both straight and bias strips.

Cutting straight strips

1. Draw straight lines at intervals across your fabric. They can be drawn lengthways or widthways and can be any width, depending on your project.

2. Using a pair of sharp dressmaking shears or a rotary cutter, cut up the strips of fabric.

Cutting bias strips

1. Cut out a square of fabric (a minimum of 50cm/20in square is best) with a selvedge on one edge.

2. Fold the opposite corners together to form a triangle and press the crease created. This will be at a 45-degree angle and on the bias grain.

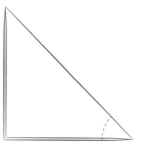

3. Open out the square and draw parallel lines diagonally at intervals across the fabric. The distance between each will vary depending on your project. I usually cut 4cm (1¾in) strips to cover piping cord for a piped cushion, for instance (see page 180). Cut with a sharp pair of dressmaking shears or a rotary cutter.

Joining the strips

Whether you're joining straight or crossways strips, it's a good idea to join them on the bias as it helps displace the bulk of the joins – when you fold the binding over, the seam folds in a different direction on either side.

1. Place two strips right sides together and at right-angles, with ends aligning. Using small stitches, machine the ends together diagonally.

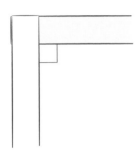

2. Trim the corners of the strips above the seam.

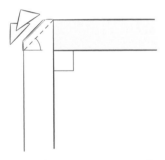

3. Press the seam open with an iron and cut the ends flush with the strip. Continue to join strips together until you have a long strip to the required length.

USING A BIAS BINDING & TAPE MAKER

This is a fabulous gadget that is very straightforward to operate. It will make bias or straight binding with turned-under edges in a multitude of widths. I have a selection in a range of sizes; the one that makes 2.5cm (1in) bias or straight binding is the one I use most. I keep the piece of card with the measurements of the different widths of fabric required for each size of maker safely stowed in a box with the gadgets!

How to operate

1. Cut strips of fabric, straight or on the bias (see opposite), for the correct width for the binding maker that you are using. (For the 2.5cm/1in machine, for instance, you'd cut widths 5cm/2in wide.) Join and press all seams, following the instructions given opposite.

2. Feed one end of the fabric into the binding maker using an awl or a pin to coax it through. Pin this first end to your ironing board.

3. Pull the binding maker by the handle while ironing the folded fabric as it comes out of the gadget. Magic! You've made some lovely binding to match your project.

USING BIAS TAPE AS AN EDGE BINDING OR FACING

1. Open out one of the folds of the binding and place right sides together on the edge to be bound. Machine along the first crease.

2. Turn over to the wrong side of the fabric and slip-stitch the second fold into the row of machining just sewn.

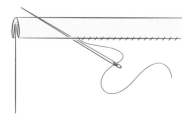

3. Alternatively, attach the right side of the binding to the wrong side of the edge to be bound. Machine along the first crease. Turn to the right side of the fabric and topstitch along the second folded edge on the right side.

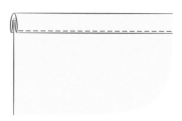

4. To use bias binding as a facing (see page 97), first follow step 1 and then turn all of the strip to the wrong side of the garment and machine in place.

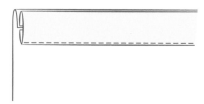

DOUBLE BINDING A CORNER

You are never too old to learn! This technique was shown to me by one of my students who was finishing a piece of patchwork. It is a fantastic way of finishing the edges of quilts and place mats (see page 128). Using this method, beautiful mitred corners are created by careful folding.

1. Cut straight strips of fabric (see page 104) 7.5cm (3in) wide. Fold each strip in half lengthways, wrong sides together, and press.

2. Position the binding on the right side of the mat or quilt so that you have a 2.5cm (1in) extension beyond the first corner.

3. Start machining the binding 5mm (¼in) from the raw edge.

4. When the stitching is 5cm (2in) from the opposite corner, insert a pin 5mm (¼in) from the corner. Stop stitching when you reach the pin and remove it. Leaving the machine needle inserted in the fabric, lift the presser foot and turn the fabric so that it is at right-angles to the row of machining. Lower the presser foot and reverse back to the raw edge.

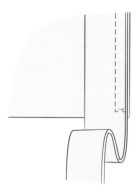

5. Take your binding strip and fold it away from you, creating a 45-degree angle to the corner.

6. Fold the binding strip back towards you, covering this 45-degree fold and aligning the new fold with the raw edge; the raw edge of the binding strip will align with the next side of the mat or quilt.

7. Starting at the corner, machine the binding 5mm (¼in) from edge, as in step 3. Continue until you reach the fourth corner.

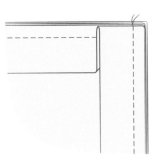

8. Stop machining 5cm (2in) from this last corner. Fold the strip that was at the beginning of your sewing away from you, creating a 45-degree angle to the corner.

9. Lay the strip you have been sewing on top and machine the ends of these strips together as near to the cut edge as you can. You may wish to turn this corner over so that you can see where all the edges are.

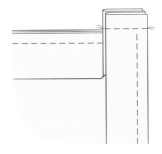

10. Trim the edges back to this row of machining. When you pull the binding away from the mat ready to wrap around the edges, ou will see four beautiful mitred corners.

11. Fold the binding under, wrapping it round the edges of the mat or quilt. Fold the mitres on the back of the corners of the binding, then hand-stitch into the row of machining on the back of the mat or quilt.

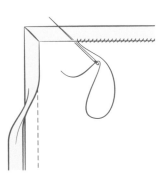

5/10

"Use *bias-cut strips* for rouleaux —

THEY FORM *MUCH SMOOTHER,* NEATER LOOPS."

PRINTED PATTERN

4011

WOMEN'S AND MISSES' DRESS

BUST

MAGIC ROULEAUX

Rouleaux are used in many different ways – on lingerie and evening wear, as ties on bags and other craft items, or to make button loops on a fine garment like a wedding dress. They can be made from cotton or silk; heavier fabrics wouldn't be suitable as they would be challenging to turn through.

BASIC ROULEAU

1. Select a piece of piping cord the same diameter as your finished rouleau strap.

2. Cut a bias strip of fabric (see page 104) wide enough to wrap around the cord and give a seam allowance.

3. Wrap the strip around the cord with the right side of the fabric facing the cord and machine or hand-stitch the top of the strip onto the cord. Using a zipper foot, machine along the strip of fabric using the cord as a guide for your sewing.

4. Pull the cord out of the tube, turning the fabric right side out in the process, and cut away the cord where it attaches to the tube. You have created a beautiful, even, and now empty, tube.

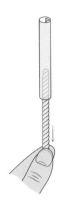

SUPER-FINE ROULEAU

Very fine tubes may be created in the same way as the basic rouleau strap. A colleague showed me a wonderful way to do this.

1. Fold the bias strip of fabric in half right sides together and machine as close to the folded edge as you dare.

2. Make a tiny snip about 5mm (¼in) from the end of the tube on the folded side and insert a hair grip into the hole.

3. Feed the clip through the tube using it to turn the tube out. The finest rouleau strap can be created this way – now that is magic!

TECHNIQUES

REINFORCED ROULEAU

Creating a tube of fabric with cord left inside it makes for a more substantial rouleau. You could use it for button loops, for instance, as I've done on my Cape (see page 212).

1. Cut a bias strip of fabric wide enough to wrap round the piping cord of your choice plus seam allowance.

2. Cut a length of cord twice the length of the bias. Wrap the fabric around the cord, with the right side facing inwards, and attach to the middle of the cord with a few machine stitches.

3. Using a zipper foot, machine along the fabric close to the cord. Trim the seam to 3mm (⅛in).

4. Pull the fabric tube right side out over the other section of cord to cover it, then cut off the excess cord. You now have a rouleau strap reinforced by piping cord.

VARIATION

✕ Rouleaux made in different colours and plaited together would make a striking alternative to the straps used for my Boned Bodice (see page 240).

ATTACHING LACE

A simple and effective way to add a decorative finish to the edges of plain lingerie. You could use the same technique for applying lace to a whole range of other items, too, from nightwear to cushions or the hem of little girl's dress.

1. Overlap the lace on the right side of the garment with the outer lace edge level with the edge of the garment.

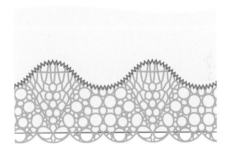

2. Zigzag the upper edge of the lace into position with matching thread.

3. Trim the fabric back to the lower edge of the zigzag stitching on the wrong side of the garment. Look at how your underwear is finished!

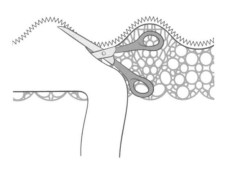

COVERING BUTTONS

Covered buttons make a fabulous finishing touch to any item, whether a garment, piece of craftwork or soft furnishing. I've used them on my Wrapped Cushion Cover on page 172, for instance, cutting out circles of fabric with star shapes in the middle to create a matching motif for each button. To make this sort of button, you need to buy a button-covering kit in the right size for your project – these are easily available and very inexpensive. If you have a lot of buttons to cover, using a button-covering gadget to press on the bottom sections of the buttons – rather than banging them on with the end of a cotton reel, as you're instructed to do in the kits – can save time and effort. I've given instructions for using this gadget, although the first three steps are the same if you're using a button-covering kit.

1. Cut out a circle of fabric the right size to cover your button – there will be a template for this in the pack.

2. Using double thread, fasten on securely and work a row of small running stitches around the edge of the circle.

3. Slip the button mould into the circle of fabric and pull the gathering thread so that the fabric hugs the mould tightly.

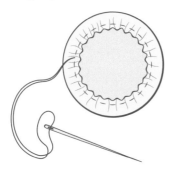

4. Place the button mould, fabric side down, in the soft side of the gadget, then position the back section of the button on top of the mould.

5. Take your needle through the hole in the back of the button and pull the thread tight.

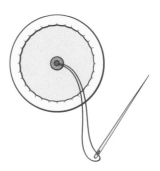

6. Place the top section of the gadget on top and press hard until the front and back of the gadget have snapped together. You now have a beautiful button with a double thread attached ready to sew on.

When I am making lots of covered buttons (26 for a valance recently!), I leave the needles attached to the buttons for sewing them on. It saves loads of time re-threading needles.

SEWING ON A BUTTON WITH A SHANK

Buttons with a shank are very useful on thicker garments to create a bit of a gap between the button and the garment so that the button lies better and is not too tightly fixed whenthe garment is fastened – less likely to pop off, too! Some buttons come with a ready-made shank (such as the covered buttons opposite), but you can create one yourself. Here's how to do it:

1. Place a cocktail stick or a matchstick on top of your button and sew over it several times through the holes of the buttons as you attach the button to the item.

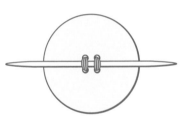

2. Remove the cocktail stick, then wind the thread from the needle around the thread attaching the button to strengthen it and make a 'stem' for the button.

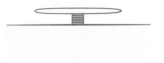

INSERTING & ALTERING ZIPS

INSERTING A ZIP

I've inserted a zip in various of my projects and given full instructions there, so do refer to these. For a semi-concealed zip, see my Pencil Skirt (page 230), and for an invisible zip see the Shift Dress (page 226). For inserting a zip in a cushion, along a straight edge – see the Piped Cushion on page 180.

SHORTENING A ZIP

If you do not have a zip the right length, it is really easy to shorten one that is longer than you need. Using a zigzag machine foot and zigzag stitch (set to stitch length zero and to maximum width), make a new bar at the requisite point on the zip to stop the pulley coming off the zip, then trim off the surplus just below the new bar.

CENTRED OR
SEMI-CONCEALED ZIP

This is a good zip insertion on the centre back of a garment. I have also used it in the back strip of my Boxed Cushion (page 175).

1. Using a pin, mark the point where the base of the zip will be positioned. Taking a 1.5cm (⅝in) seam allowance, stitch the seam to this point. Press the seam open, including the unstitched section, and neaten the edges.

2. Position the zip so that the tape at the top is level with the raw edge and the fold in the left-hand seam allowance covers the teeth on the left side of the zip. Pin and tack the zip in place.

3. Butt the second seamline fold up against the first, so that the zip is completely covered. Pin and tack the zip in place.

4. Place a piece of 3mm (⅛in) masking tape 6mm (¼in) away from the seamline fold on both sides of the zip. This will act as a handy stitching guide.

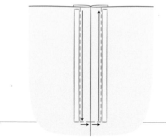

5. Attach a zipper foot to your machine. Starting at the top of the left-hand side and stitching down the inside edge of the masking tape, machine the zip in place. When you reach the bottom of the first side, leave the needle down in the fabric, turn, count the number of stitches you take up to the fold on the seam allowance, and then make the same number of stitches on the other side (this will aid symmetry). Machine up the second side, again along the inside edge of the masking tape. Remove the masking tape and tacking stitches, and press.

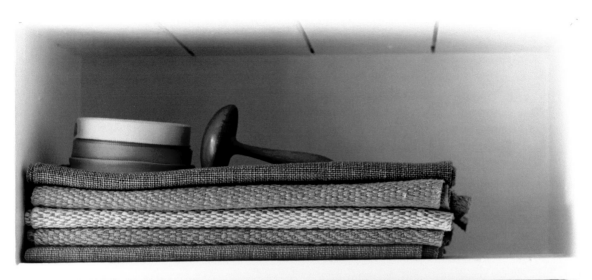

TECHNIQUES

QUILTING

Quilts were worked by hand originally, of course, although using a sewing machine makes the process a great deal quicker. They are usually worked through three layers (as I've done for the Log Cabin Place Mat on page 128):

The top layer – the right side, comprising patchwork, appliqué or patterned fabric.

The middle layer – consisting of wadding or batting, which comes in different weights and is made from different fibres.

The backing layer – usually muslin, cotton or calico.

STARTING TO QUILT

1. Pin and tack the layers together, starting from the centre and working outwards. On larger projects, use safety pins to hold the layers together.

2. Quilt by hand using small running stitches or by machine using a slightly larger straight stitch than you would use for seaming (test stitches on a sample piece. The size of the stitching depending on how many layers you're working (for more layers you'll need a larger stitch).

3. To work parallel lines, a quilting guide (see page 57) can be attached to the foot of your sewing machine; alternatively, lines of quilter's masking tape can be laid along the surface of the fabric. Use a walking or even feed foot on your sewing machine.

PAPER-BACKED FUSIBLE WEB

Paper-backed fusible web, such as Bondaweb, is an incredibly versatile product for gluing shapes permanently to other fabric for functional or decorative purposes. It consists of a fine web-like layer of glue supported by a layer of silicone paper. The texture on one surface feels rough to touch – this is the glue, which melts when heated with an iron. To avoid sticky deposits on your ironing board, it is a good idea to cover it with an oven liner and press with greaseproof paper on top of your appliqué design or repair patch.

APPLIQUÉ

1. Cut a square of fusible web slightly bigger than the finished shape to be applied. Iron this square on to the wrong side of a slightly bigger piece of fabric.

2. Draw your shape on the backing paper, bearing in mind that you are drawing the back of the shape. If you are making letters, for instance (such as for the Puppet Theatre on page 140), remember to draw them back to front!

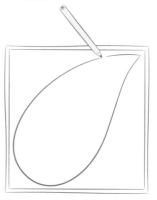

3. Cut out the shape and peel off the backing paper.

4. Position the shape on the background fabric glue side down and then bond into position with either a steam iron or through damp muslin.

5. Stitch around the edge of the shape to attach firmly in place with either a satin stitch (close zigzag), zigzag stitch or any other decorative stitch.

Stitching fusible web

Bonding the shapes can make them stiff and make the machine needle sticky with glue. The work may also need to be supported by an extra layer of fabric or a layer of Stitch and Tear (a Vilene product with a paper-like feel). If the machine needle sticks, change it for a new one.

FUNCTIONAL USES

Paper-backed fusible web is ideal for repairing rips and holes in clothing and other items.

Invisible repairs

1. Iron a square or rectangle of fusible web on to the front or right side of a piece of fabric matching in colour and texture to the item being repaired. Peel off the paper backing and iron the piece of fabric onto the back of the rip or tear.

2. On the front or right side of the fabric, machine darn with matching thread in the same direction as the grain of the fabric.

Patches

Children's trouser knees are a classic example of where a patch can be used:

1. Follow steps 1 and 2 for appliqué, then peel off the paper backing and iron the piece of fabric to the right side of the garment.

2. Zigzag round the edges of the patch to finish.

MILWARDS
GOLD SEAL
BEST QUALITY NEEDLES
MADE IN REDDITCH, ENGLAND

NEEDLES
OVER A CENTURY'S
REPUTATION

SWISS
SARSNETS
Nº 2

DO NOT OPEN UNTIL
25
DECEMBER

Chez MONNERET ET DUSSERRE à Lyon.   8 cm

Lusta
HOSEDARN

MERCERISED LISLE
· SHADE No. 77 ·
BRITISH AND BEST

CRAFTS

CRAFTS

TABLE RUNNER

This runner, which will bring instant glamour to your table, is really simple to create. It makes an elegant addition to a meal setting and is a lovely way of dressing a table at other times, perhaps with a bowl of fruit on top. I've used cotton here, but it would look gorgeous in raw silk – just be careful not to spill anything on it!

YOU WILL NEED
Main fabric: 1.5m x 50cm (1⅝yd x 20in) cotton
Thread: All-purpose sewing thread
Accessories: Two 5cm (2in) tassels

ASSEMBLY

1. Fold the fabric in half lengthways, right sides together. Pin the edges together and then machine-stitch along the long raw edge, 1cm (½in) from the edge.

2. Press the seam open, using a cardboard tube under the seam in order not to flatten the rest of the runner (see page 22).

3. Adjust the tube of fabric so that the seam runs along the centre of the back of the runner. Pin and machine-stitch across one short end 1cm (½in) from the raw edge. Pin and stitch the other short end, leaving an 8cm (3in) gap in the middle for turning out.

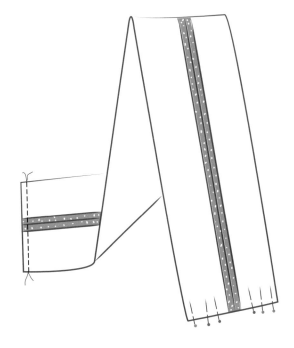

4. Turn the fabric right side out through the gap, pushing the corners out with a chopstick or a point turner.

5. Press all the edges, making sure that edges of the gap are folded in, then slip-stitch the gap closed.

7. Tuck the cord of one of the tassels between the edges near one of the points and slip-stitch the edges together, catching the tassel in place. Repeat with the other tassel. Turn over to hide the seams, then place along the centre of your table and enjoy!

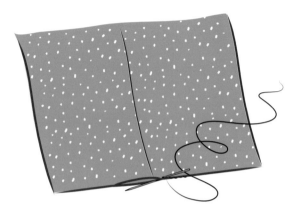

6. With the seam facing you, fold in both corners at one end of the runner to meet on the seam, creating a point. Press with the iron, then repeat with the corners at the other end of the runner.

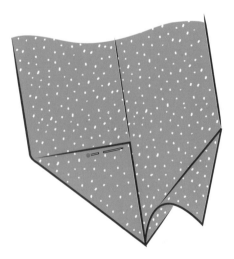

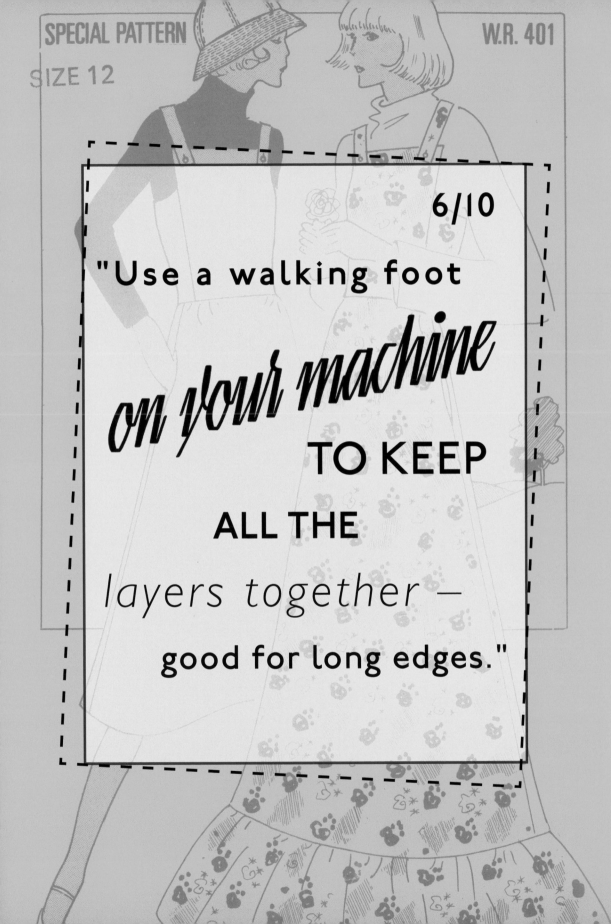

6/10

"Use a walking foot *on your machine* TO KEEP ALL THE *layers together —* good for long edges."

CRAFTS

No.2

NAPKINS &
NAPKIN RINGS

Coordinating napkins and napkin rings add the perfect finishing touch to any table. Not only are they inexpensive to make, but they can be designed to suit your colour scheme or made in bright colours for Christmas or other festive occasions.

YOU WILL NEED

Template: Tracing paper
　　Empty cereal packet
Main fabric: Im (I⅛yd) cotton, II5cm
　　(45in) wide, for four napkins
Contrast fabric: 20cm (8in) cotton,
　　II5cm (45in) wide, for the rose motifs
　　I5cm (6in) cotton fabric, II5cm (45in) wide, for
　　four napkin rings
Interfacing: I0cm (4in) square of heavyweight
　　sew-in interfacing (such as Vilene)
Thread: All-purpose sewing thread
Accessories: 50cm (20in) fusible buckram, I3cm
　　(5in) wide
　　Fabric glue or glue gun

CUTTING OUT AND ASSEMBLY

Napkins

1. Cut out four 50cm (20in) squares from the fabric.

2. Follow the instructions on page 90 for hemming the napkins with double-mitred corners, folding over the edges twice (by Icm/½in for the first fold and I.5cm/⅝in for the second). Use a decorative stitch on your sewing machine for the hem.

Napkin rings

1. Cut four I3.5 x I6.5cm (5¼ x 6½in) strips from the contrast fabric.

2. Cut four 6.5cm x I8cm (2½in x 7in) strips from the buckram.

3. Wrap a strip of fabric around a piece of buckram so that it meets in the centre on the back and I.5cm (⅝in) of buckram protrudes from one end (see diagram overleaf). Press in place with a steam iron or a damp cloth to fuse the buckram to the fabric, leaving Icm (½in) of the buckram unfused at the other end of the strip.

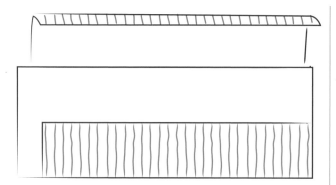

2. Make another fold 1cm (½in) deep to the right of the central fold, butting up against the first fold but not overlapping. Make another fold to the left of the central fold, again about 1cm (½in) deep and butting up against but not overlapping the central fold.

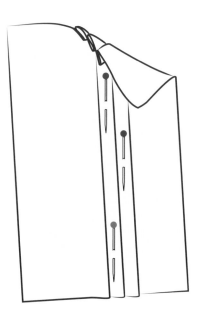

4. Tuck the protruding end of the buckram just inside the other end of the strip, and press in place to hold in a circle, using a cardboard tube to support the join (see page 22). The join will be covered when you add the rose motif. Repeat steps 3–4 to make the remaining napkin rings.

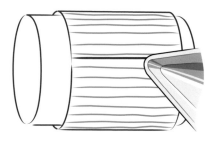

3. Turn the folded fabric 90 degrees and fold again in the same way, then press in position with an iron.

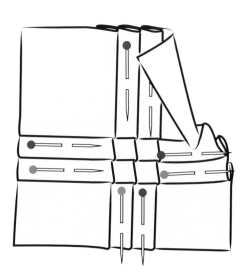

Folded rose motifs

1. Cut out four 20cm (8in) squares of fabric. With the right side facing you, make a vertical fold in the centre of one piece of fabric about 1cm (½in) deep.

4. Using the pattern provided, trace and cut out a hexagon template from the cereal-packet card, then use this to cut out four hexagons from the interfacing. Place one hexagon in the middle of the folded fabric on the wrong side. Pin in place and machine-stitch along the edge of the hexagon, as near to the edge as possible. Wrap the edges of the folded fabric around the hexagon and pin in place.

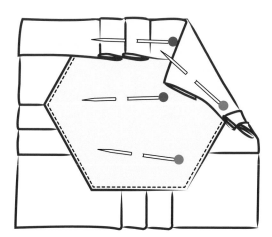

5. On the right side of the folded fabric, pull and twist the pleats to form the rose shape. Catch at intervals using hand stitches.

6. Place the rose over one of the napkin rings to cover the join and glue it into position, using fabric glue or a glue gun. Alternatively, stitch it in place by hand.

7. Repeat steps 1–6 to make the remaining rose motifs and attach them to the napkin rings.

CRAFTS

LOG CABIN PATCHWORK

Log cabin patchwork is extremely versatile and, as you will see from the projects included here, can be used to make a range of items. I've started with instructions for making a place mat to get you started, and shown below how to expand the technique for a table runner and play mat, but the variations are endless. If you're feeling ambitious, you could carry on making more squares and join them up into a bedspread!

I have chosen a pattern that looks like steps – the traditional name is 'Courthouse Steps', in fact. To create this effect, you attach contrasting strips on opposite sides of a central square, the strips on each side gradually increasing in size.

PLACE MAT

The quantities below are for one mat measuring approximately 30cm (12in) square.

YOU WILL NEED

Main fabric: 15cm (6in) each of 2 contrasting cottons, 115cm (45in) wide, for the upper side of the mat

Foundation square: 33cm (13in) square of curtain lining (or any scrap fabric you have to hand)

Backing fabric and binding: 32cm (12I/2in) cotton 115cm (45in) wide, for backing the mat and binding the finished edge

Interlining: 33cm (13in) square of lightweight polyester interlining or 70g (2oz) wadding (see tip on page 132)

Thread: All-purpose sewing thread

CUTTING OUT AND ASSEMBLY

1. Cut out an 11cm (4½in) square of fabric from one of the main fabrics, then cut the rest of these two fabrics into long strips across the width of the fabric, each strip measuring 6cm (2½in) wide (see tip on page 134).

2. Cut a 33cm (13in) square of interlining or wadding. Sandwich this together with the foundation square. (You will be working with the interlining side facing you.) Position the 11cm (4½in) square right side up in the middle of the interlining and tack it in place.

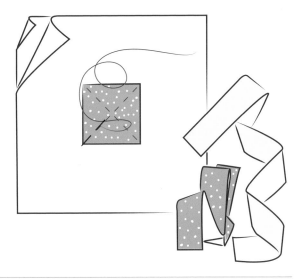

CRAFTS

3. Line up a strip of contrasting main fabric along one side of the central square, right sides together, pin in position and machine-stitch 5mm (¼in) from the edge. Cut the bottom of the strip so that it's level with the central square.

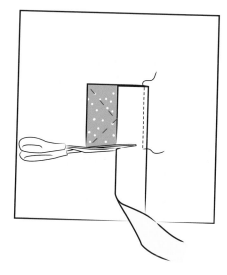

4. Flip the strip over and pin into position, with the pin tip pointing towards the raw edge of the fabric. Repeat steps 3–4 to attach a strip of fabric to the opposite side of the square.

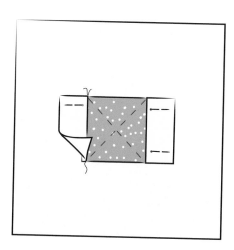

5. Using the other upper fabric to create a contrast in colour, repeat steps 3–4 to join another strip across all of these sections. Repeat on the opposite side.

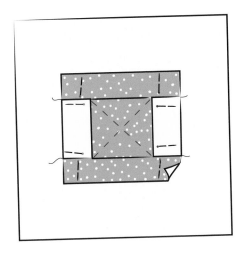

6. Continue building up the design in the same way, stitching strips to opposite sides. (There are just eight strips around the central square here, but you could keep going, following the formula above, to create a larger mat.)

7. Trim off the excess foundation square to give a 31cm (12½in) square.

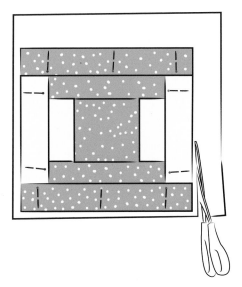

8. Cut a 31cm (12½in) square of backing fabric to hide all the machine ends. Cut the rest

of the backing fabric into strips 7.5cm (3in) wide for the binding. Place the log cabin block right side down on your work surface, with the backing square right side up on top, and pin together.

9. Double bind the edges of the place mat, following the instructions on page 106. The square of backing fabric is stitched in as you attach the binding.

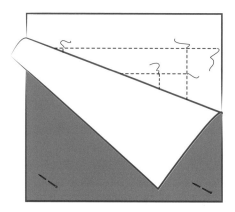

TABLE RUNNER

YOU WILL NEED

Main fabric: 50cm (⅝yd) each of 2 contrasting cottons, 115cm (45in) wide, for the upper side of the mat

Foundation squares: Three 33cm (13in) squares of curtain lining (or any scrap fabric you have to hand)

Backing fabric and binding: 70cm (28in) cotton, 115cm (45in) wide, for backing the mat and binding the edge

Interlining: 111 x 41cm (44½ x 16½in) lightweight polyester interlining or 70g (2oz) wadding

Thread: All-purpose sewing thread

CUTTING OUT AND ASSEMBLY

1. Follow the instructions for the Place Mat to make three squares, but do not incorporate any interlining or backing fabric at this stage.

2. Using one of the main fabrics, cut out four strips 6cm (2½in) wide and machine-stitch in place to join the squares together and form a border along each short side.

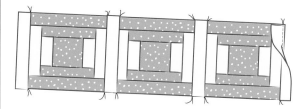

3. Cut out and machine in place two long strips in the same fabric to create a border for each of the long sides.

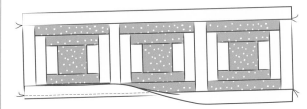

4. Cut a piece of backing fabric and a piece of interlining the same size as the patchwork. Place the backing fabric right side down on your work surface. Place the interlining on top, with the patchwork right side up on top of the interlining. Pin or tack together through all three layers. Double bind the edges, following the instructions on page 106.

Many different products are available for interlining your patchwork, including heat-resistant varieties that would be ideal for a place mat. Ask at a patchwork and quilting shop for further information.

PLAY MAT

I've given instructions here for making two versions of the Play Mat, one in the Courthouse Steps pattern used for the Place Mat and Table Runner on pages 128–132 and one in a variation of log cabin patchwork made up of concentric squares – as illustrated in the photograph on page 135. You can of course combine the strips of fabric to create designs of your own.

YOU WILL NEED

Main fabric:

Courthouse steps: 2m (2¼yd) each of 2 contrasting cottons, 115cm (45in) wide, for the upper side of the mat

Concentric squares: 1m (1⅛yd) each of 3 contrasting cottons, 115cm (45in) wide, for the upper side of mat
0.5m (½yd) cotton fabric, 115cm (45cm) wide, for the central squares (I used a fabric with animal motifs)

Foundation squares: Nine 33cm (13in) squares of curtain lining (or any scrap fabric you have to hand)

Backing fabric and binding: 1.5m (1⅝yd) cotton, 115cm (45in) wide, for backing the mat and binding the finished edge
1m (1⅛yd) cotton, 115cm (45in) wide, for the sashing strips (or use more backing fabric)

Interlining: 111cm (44½in) squre of lightweight polyester interlining or 70g (2oz) wadding

Thread: All-purpose sewing thread

CUTTING OUT AND ASSEMBLY

Courthouse steps

1. Follow the instructions for the Place Mat to make nine squares, but do not incorporate any interlining or backing fabric at this stage. Lay the squares out in three rows of three.

2. In each row, add a 6cm (2½in) wide strip on either side of the central square to join them together into a strip. Then add a longer strip between rows 1 and 2, and between rows 2 and 3, to make a square of nine blocks.

3. Add a further strip to each side of this large square, and complete the mat by adding a strip to the top and bottom.

4. Cut a square of backing fabric and a square of interlining the same size as the patchwork. Place the backing fabric right side down on your work surface. Place the interlining on top, with the patchwork right side up on top of the interlining. Pin or tack together through all three layers. Double bind the edges, following the instructions on page 106.

While not essential, a rotary cutter, ruler and cutting mat will ensure fabulous cut edges when cutting out strips of fabric.

Top Tip

Concentric squares

This Play Mat is constructed in the same way but using a different motif for each of the nine central squares. You'll need to cut the central squares (made using animal fabric in my mat) slightly smaller than those in the step design: 8.5cm (3½in) instead of 10cm (4in). Rather than putting contrasting strips on either side of each central square, you create a border of the same-coloured fabric, then swap to a different fabric for the next border, with a third border around this. Build up the strips in the same way as for the Courthhouse Steps pattern (see page 133), then assemble the play mat in exactly the same way.

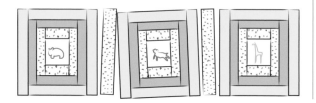

CRAFTS

CRAFTS

EXPRESS BUNTING

This is a really neat and speedy way of making lots of bunting! I made several metres recently for a special birthday party. It was a lovely sunny day and they were draped around the patio where we had lunch, adding a wonderfully festive and summery touch.

The quantities below are for just over 5m (5½yd) of bunting (28 triangles in total), though you can repeat the quantities to make as much as you like. The triangles each measure 20cm (8in) along one side, but you can follow this formula to make triangles of any size. If you would prefer to mark out triangles individually, make a template from the larger pattern provided. Equally, if you make the triangles following the method below, the larger template can be used to check your triangles are the right size as you mark up the fabric. Be sure to have the bunting diagrams by you as you read through the instructions.

YOU WILL NEED

Template: Tracing paper
  Empty cereal packet
Main fabric: 80cm (32in) of one cotton or 40cm (16in) each of two contrasting cottons, 115cm (45in) wide
Backing fabric: 80cm (32in) plain cotton, 115cm (45in) wide
Binding: 6m (6½yd) bias binding (to make your own, see page 104)
Thread: All-purpose sewing thread
Accessories (optional): Gridded ruler (see tip on page 139)
  Rotary cutter and cutting mat (see tip on page 139)

CUTTING OUT & ASSEMBLY

1. Using the pattern provided, trace and cut out the smaller triangle from the cereal-packet card. (If making up the bunting triangles individually – see introduction – trace and cut out the larger triangle from card, too.)

2. Cut one 40 x 80cm (15¾ x 31½in) piece from the main fabric (cutting the longer side from the width of the fabric) and a similar-sized piece from the backing fabric.

3. On the wrong side of the backing fabric, mark the central point of each short edge (20cm/8in from each long edge) with a chalk pencil, then, using your ruler, draw a line running down the centre of the fabric. To ensure that the line remains straight – 20cm (8in) from each side – it's a good idea to mark further points along the fabric before drawing the line.

4. Starting from one corner of the fabric, make marks at 20cm (8in) intervals along each long edge.

5. Starting at one corner, draw a diagonal line (angled at 60 degrees) from here to the first 20cm (8in) point on the other long side, then draw further diagonal lines parallel to the first one and at the same angle across the fabric.

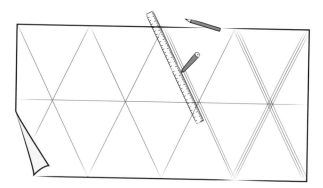

6. Draw lines across in the other direction to create a series of triangles for the bunting. All of these lines (marked as blue lines in the diagram) are for cutting along, so you now need to draw lines at 5mm (¼in) on either side for machine-sewing along (marked as red lines in the diagram).

7. Put the backing fabric and main fabric right sides together and machine-stitch along the red lines, stitching diagonally first in one direction and then in the other.

8. Cut along the blue lines (a rotary cutter is ideal for this purpose) to make 14 triangles.

9. Turn the fabric triangles right side out. Insert the smaller cardboard triangle inside one of the cloth triangles and, using an iron, press with the card in place - it will help push the shape out. Press the remaining triangles in the same way.

10. Using the remaining pieces of backing and main fabric, repeat steps 2–9.

Making the bunting

1. Leaving 30cm (12in) free at each end of the binding (for tying up the finished bunting), open out one folded edge and lay this on top of the open edge of one of the triangles. Line up the edges and pin into position. Repeat with all the remaining triangles, butting them up against each other and pinning into position.

2. Machine-stitch along the crease on the binding to sew the triangles into position.

3. Fold the binding in half and machine in place with a decorative stitch such as a three-step zigzag so that you can be sure of catching the other side of the binding. The binding can be stitched with a straight stitch, but it is more difficult to make sure that you catch the other side of the fabric.

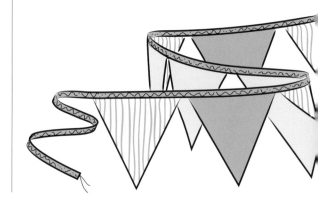

CRAFTS

VARIATIONS

✕ You can ring the changes for this bunting – using more than two types of patterned fabric for the front and back of the triangles, for instance, or alternating lots of different-coloured triangles when you sew the bunting together. It's a great way of using up any scraps of material that you have to hand.

Choose fabric that is multi-directional and this method will make lots of bunting very quickly. A rotary cutter and gridded ruler with angles marked are very useful for this project, although you could use a standard ruler and protractor otherwise. It's important that the triangles are each measured precisely or the whole grid will become skewed.

CRAFTS

DOORWAY PUPPET THEATRE

Over ten years ago, a student of mine brought in a tiny picture from a magazine showing what looked like a doorway puppet theatre. We made it for her daughter, who is now 14, and Mum still has it! The beauty of this little theatre is that it requires no complicated stand but can be suspended on hooks in a doorway for the puppeteers to perform a show. To make your own puppets to go with the theatre, see the Hand Puppets on page 146. Combining both projects is wonderful for developing a child's imagination – and a lot of fun for adults too!

YOU WILL NEED

Templates: Tracing paper
   2 empty cereal packets
Main fabric: 1m (1⅛yd) striped cotton, 115cm
   (45in) wide, for the curtains and scalloped
   edge
   2m (2¼yd) strong cotton (I used denim that
   was 152cm/60in wide – see tip on page 144)
Fabric for details: 40 x 115cm (16 x 45in) spotted
   cotton for the bunting, tie-backs and letters
   15 x 48cm (6 x 19in) each of two contrasting
   plain cottons for the remaining butning
   triangles
Thread: All-purpose sewing thread
Accessories: 1m (1⅛yd) paper-backed fusible
   web for the appliqué detail
   116cm (46in) curtain-heading tape, 2.5cm
   (1in) wide
   2 eyelets and 2 hooks
   2 lengths of dowelling

CUTTING OUT AND ASSEMBLY

Bottom panel

1. Using the pattern supplied, trace and cut out the scallop template from the cereal-packet card. Repeat for the letters needed for the words 'PUPPET SHOW'.

2. Cut a 30 x 80cm (12 x 32in) strip from the striped fabric and fold it in half across the width of the fabric (so that the stripes appear vertically in the finished scalloping), with the right sides together.

3. Position the straight edge of the scallop template 1.5cm (⅝in) away from the open edge and draw round it using a chalk pencil. Draw a series of scallop shapes along the length of the fabric, then machine-stitch along these lines, following the instructions on page 90. You can use the scallop

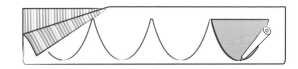

template for pushing out the shapes before ironing them.

4. Cut a 71cm (28in) length from the strong cotton. With the right side of both fabrics uppermost and starting 1cm (½in) from the side, position the finished scalloped edge along one half of the width of the fabric so that the tops align. Pin and machine-stitch in place.

5. Fold over the other half of the strong cotton, enclosing the scalloped edge, and machine the side and the edge with the scalloping.

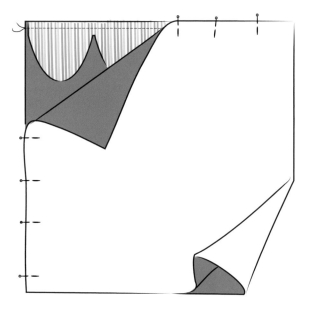

6. Turn through and press. Pin together and zigzag the raw edges of the completed bottom panel.

7. Using the letter templates, trace, cut out and apply the words 'PUPPET SHOW' following the instructions for appliqué on page 116). (You could use different types of fabric here if you liked, in alternating colours.)

Side panels

Cut out two 54cm (21in) squares of the strong cotton. Fold each in half lengthways (along the grain of the fabric), with right sides together, to create the narrow side panels, then pin and machine the vertical seam on each. Turn each section through to the right side and press the seam on the edge.

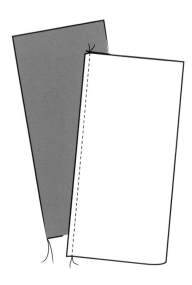

Top panel

1. Cut a 57cm (22½in) length of strong cotton. Fold in half, right sides together, then pin and machine along the top and down the side. Turn through and press, then pin together and zigzag the raw edges.

2. Using the pattern supplied, trace, draw and cut out the bunting template from the cereal-packet card and use this for marking and cutting out nine triangles from the three different 'detail' fabrics. (As with the letters, you can play around with different fabric combinations here.)

3. Decorate the top panel with mock bunting, following the appliqué instructions on page 116.

Curtains

1. Cut a 70cm (27½in) length from the striped
   fabric (effectively most of the remaining
   fabric minus the section not used for the
   scalloped edge) and cut in half lengthways
   (so that the stripes appear vertically in the
   finished curtains) to give you two curtain
   pieces each 70cm (27½in) long and 57.5cm
   (23in) wide. On every side of each piece,
   fold over the edges to the wrong side by 1cm
   (½in) and by 2cm (¾in) again to make small
   hems, then machine in place and press.

2. Pin a piece of heading tape to the top of
   each curtain piece, on the wrong side, and
   machine into position.

Assembling the theatre

1. Take the top panel, fold under 6cm (2½in) of
   the zigzagged lower edge to the wrong side
   and press. Pin this to the top edge of each of
   the side panels (with the seams of the side
   panels on the outside edges) and machine
   in place to create the theatre opening with
   a tuck or casing into which a length of
   dowelling can later be inserted to reinforce
   the structure.

2. Repeat step 1 for the bottom panel.

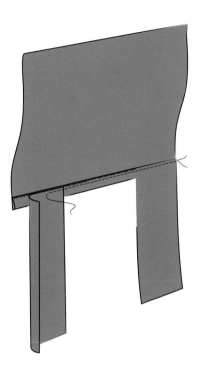

3. Cut two 62 x 5cm (24 x 2in) strips for the
   tie-backs. Fold each piece of fabric in
   half lengthways, right sides together, and
   machine along three sides, leaving a 5cm
   (2in) gap in the middle of the long edge.
   Turn right side out and press, then slip-
   stitch the gap closed.

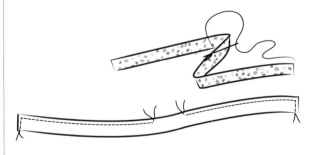

4. Attach each tie-back about halfway up each
   side panel on the front and 5cm (2in) from
   the edge of the theatre opening.

5. Gather each curtain using the heading tape and arrange them over the opening so that they just meet in the middle. Pin to the upper panel and machine in place. Tie each curtain back and insert a length of dowelling into each casing above and below the theatre opening.

If you cannot find denim or other strong cotton as wide as 152cm (60in), adjust the measurements to fit the width of your fabric. Be sure to use a strong 'jeans' needle on your sewing machine when working with a tough fabric like denim.

Attaching to a doorway

Make eyelet holes in the top corners of door theatre following the manufacturer's instructions, then screw two hooks in a convenient place on a doorway frame and hook the theatre onto them.

CRAFTS

CRAFTS

HAND PUPPETS

These puppets are such fun to make as well as being perfect for use with the Doorway Puppet Theatre on page 140. I have included several puppet patterns, all of which you can customise to suit, using different colours of felt and varying the accessories. I am going to give you assembly details for the City Mouse to get you started, but the other puppets can all be made in pretty much the same way as they all use the same basic body shape. Having made one or two of these, you may be inspired to create your own designs – the only restrictions are your imagination!

YOU WILL NEED

Templates: Tracing paper
    Empty cereal packet
Main fabric: Two 30cm (12in) squares of felt for
    the puppet body
Fabric for details: Offcuts of felt in
    coordinating colours for the other parts of
    the puppet
Threads: All-purpose sewing thread
    Stranded black embroidery thread for the
    mouth and whiskers
Needle: Crewel needle for embroidering
Accessories: 30cm (12in) ribbon, 2.5cm
    (1in) wide
    2 buttons
    Fabric glue (see tip on page 149)

CUTTING OUT

City Mouse parts

1. Using the patterns at the back of the book, trace and cut out the larger and smaller body templates from card. Place the larger template on each of the squares of felt in turn and draw around it with a chalk pencil to make two body pieces, then cut these out.

2 Using the patterns provided, trace and cut out one face piece and two outer ear pieces in the same colour of felt as the body. (I used grey felt, but mice come in different colours!)

3. Cut out two inner ear pieces, a nose and eight paw pieces in a contrasting colour. (I used pink here.)

4. Cut out the eyes and the main section of the bowler hat in the same colour of felt. (I used black felt.)

5. Cut out two waistcoat pieces in a strongly contrasting colour of felt. In the same colour, cut out four little strips of felt for the pocket flaps (two smaller and two larger) and the band for the hat.

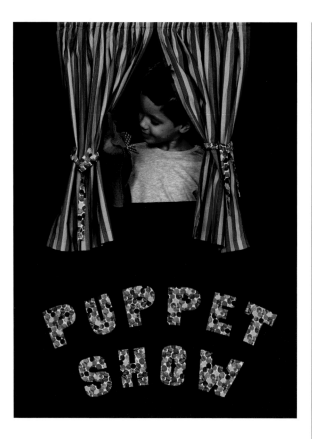

ASSEMBLY

1. Glue the pocket flaps to the waistcoat. Pin the body pieces together, with the waistcoat pieces on top, and machine-stitch around them, 5mm (¼in) from the edges, leaving the bottom edges open.

2. Insert the smaller card template into the body – this is to stop the back and front sections from sticking together while you are gluing on the mouse's clothes and other body parts. Stick the eyes, nose, hat and fringe in position, using the photo on page 146 as a guide.

3. Draw the mouth and, using embroidery thread, chain-stitch along the line (see box). Use long straight stitches either side of the nose to make the whiskers.

4. Stick the paw, ear and hat pieces in position, then sew on the buttons. Tie the ribbon in a bow and attach with glue or a couple of stitches at the neck.

VARIATIONS

✕ You could use pinking shears to cut out the puppet body. This would be good option if you use fabric other than felt for making the puppets.

✕ The puppets' features can look just as effective drawn in black felt tip.

✕ Templates for the Sleepy Mouse, Clown and Owl Puppets can be found at the back of the book.

Use good-quality glue and a fresh tube of it – not one you have had in the cupboard for a long time!

CHAIN STITCH

1. Thread a crewel needle with 2–3 threads from an embroidery skein. Bring the needle up to the front of the fabric at A. Take it down at B (next to the point at which it first emerged), then bring it up again at C, looping the thread under the needle tip. Pull the needle through.

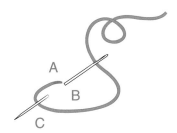

2. Insert the needle at C and bring it up at D, again looping the thread under the needle tip. Continue in this way until you reach the end of the stitching line, then take the needle over the last loop to the back of the fabric and finish off securely.

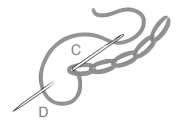

CRAFTS

CHRISTMAS DECORATIONS

I originally saw these in a Japanese folded-patchwork book and thought they would make lovely Christmas decorations. All the family and many friends are now the proud owners of these simple but effective decorations – you don't even need a sewing machine to make the Hexagon Star. As only a small amount of fabric is needed (unless you're making a large number of each), you could use any scraps you have to hand for this. Alternatively, you could buy ready-cut squares of fabric from patchwork and quilting shops.

HEXAGON STAR

YOU WILL NEED
Template: Tracing paper
   Empty cereal packet
Main fabric: 25 x 14cm (10 x 5½in) cotton
Contrast fabric: 25 x 10cm (10 x 4in) cotton
Interfacing: 20 x 10cm (8 x 4in) fusible
   interfacing (such as Vilene)
Thread: All-purpose sewing thread
Accessories: 12 beads
   1 x 20cm (8in) ribbon, 1cm (½in) wide

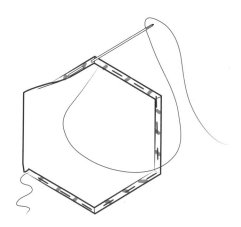

CUTTING OUT AND ASSEMBLY

1. Using the patterns provided, trace and cut out one large and one small hexagon from cereal-packet card.

2. Place the larger hexagon template on the main fabric, draw around the shape using a chalk pencil and cut it out.

3. Fold over the six edges to the wrong side of the fabric by 2–3mm/⅛in.

4. Iron the interfacing onto the contrast piece of fabric and use the smaller hexagon template to draw around and cut out two hexagons.

5. Place one small hexagon on top of a large one, wrong sides together and angled as in the diagram overleaf. Secure in place with a pin if necessary. Fold over the corners of the larger hexagon as shown overleaf, and secure each of the six tips with a hand stitch or two and a bead.

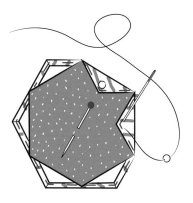

6. Repeat steps 2–5 to make a second star.

7. Fold the ribbon in half to form a loop and stitch it to the back of one of the stars for hanging the decoration.

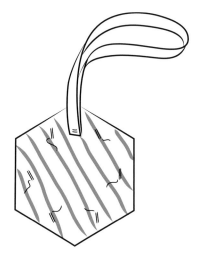

8. Place the two hexagon stars back to back, offset as shown, so that one set of points is in between the other. Secure the stars to each other with a few hand stitches.

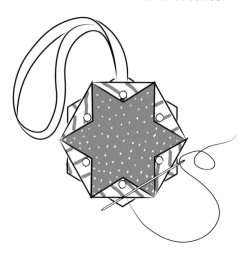

FIELD FLOWER

YOU WILL NEED

Template: Tracing paper
    Empty cereal packet
Main fabric: 25 x 15cm (10 x 6in) cotton
Contrast fabric: 25 x 15cm (10 x 6in) cotton
Thread: All-purpose sewing thread
Accessories: 15cm (6in) ribbon, 1cm (⅜in) wide

CUTTING OUT AND ASSEMBLY

1. Using the template on page 299, trace and cut out a circle from cereal-packet card.

2. Place the main and contrast fabrics right sides together. Using a chalk pencil, draw around the circle template twice, leaving space in between.

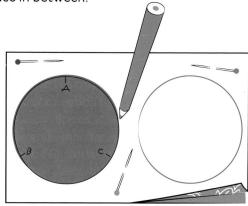

3. Machine stitch along the drawn lines, reducing the length of the stitch to make it easier to go around the curves. Cut out, cutting 3mm (⅛in) from the stitching.

4. Take one circle and, on the main side of the fabric, cut a very small cross in the middle, taking care to cut only through the top layer of fabric. Use this gap to turn the circle right side out. Use a chopstick or point turner, inserted through the cut, to push the seam to the edge, then press flat.

CRAFTS

5. Use the circle template to mark points A, B and C, marking each point with a pin. Fold across between two pins, so that the edge of the circle touches the centre and secure with a few hand stitches.

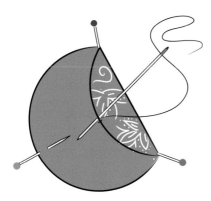

6. Fold back and secure the remaining two flaps of the flower in the same way.

7. Press the folded-down flaps into position. Press the overlapping edges of each flap back to create the petal shape.

8. Repeat steps 5–7 to make the second flower. (You could snip the cross in the circle made from the contrast fabric this time, if you liked, and fold over the main fabric for this flower.)

9. Fold the ribbon in half to form a loop and stitch it to the back of one of the flowers for hanging the finished decoration.

10. Place the two flowers back to back, angled to form a six-pointed shape, and secure with a few hand stitches to create a beautiful double-sided flower.

VARIATIONS

✕ Made up in different-coloured fabric, these would make lovely decorations for Mother's Day or Easter, when they could be suspended from branches with a few painted eggs.
✕ Several of both types of decoration could be made (minus any beads) in bright colours, and/or different sizes and assembled to make a child's mobile.

CRAFTS

CHRISTMAS STOCKING

Every child needs a Christmas stocking, and a home-made one is so much better than anything you can buy in the shops. My granddaughter was the latest recipient of this very simple design. I have used Makower ticking in red for this project, but any Christmas-themed fabric would do.

YOU WILL NEED

Template: Tracing paper
    Greaseproof paper for pattern
Main fabric: 60cm (24in) cotton, 115cm
    (45in) wide, for the stocking
Lining: 40cm (16in) lining fabric, 137cm (54in)
    wide, (such as polyester and cotton curtain
    lining)
Fabric for details: two 20cm (8in) lengths of
    cotton for the star, heel and toe
Interlining: 40cm (16in) interlining (see tip
    on page 157)
Thread: All-purpose sewing thread
Accessories: 50cm (20in) paper-backed
    fusible web
    120cm (8in) ribbon, 1.5cm (⅝in) wide

Top Tip

Use polyester and cotton curtain lining and synthetic interlinings as they are 137cm (54in) wide and economical to use.

CUTTING OUT

1. Using the patterns provided, trace and cut out templates from greaseproof paper for the stocking shape, inner and outer stars, heel and toe.

2. Following steps 1 and 2 for 'Appliqué' (page 116), draw the star, heel and toe on the fusible web and then iron them on to the detail fabrics – using one fabric for the heel, toe and inner star and the other fabric for the outer star. Cut out the shapes but don't peel off the backing paper.

3. Use the stocking template to draw and cut out two stocking shapes in the main fabric, lining and interlining, either folding the fabric in half and cutting through two layers at once, or flipping the template over before you draw the second stocking, so that you get a left and a right stocking.

ASSEMBLY

1. Tack a piece of interlining to the wrong side of each stocking piece. (The interlining will support the outer fabric when you attach the toe, heel and star motifs.)

2. Apply the toe, heel and star motifs to the right side of one of the outer stocking pieces, following steps 3–5 for 'Appliqué' on page 116.

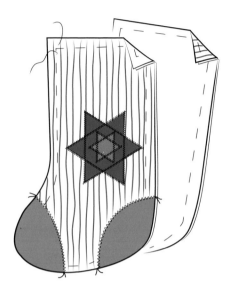

3. Place both outer stocking pieces right sides together and machine-stitch 1cm (½in) in from the edge, leaving the top edges open. Trim the interlining back to just beyond the stitching, trim the seam allowances of the outer fabric back to 5mm (¼in) and snip the inner curves (see page 84). Turn right side out.

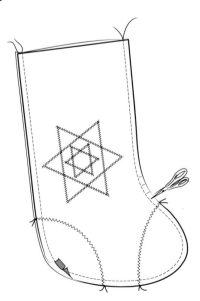

4. Place both lining pieces right sides together and machine around the edges, leaving the top open and a 10cm (4in) gap in the back seam for turning the stocking through. Trim the seam allowances of the lining fabric to 5mm (¼in) and snip the inner curves.

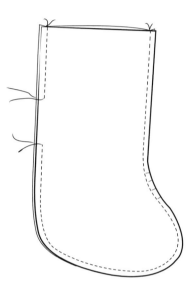

5. Fold the ribbon into a loop and pin to the outer stocking with the raw edges level with the top of the stocking and the loop lying along the back seam of the stocking. Machine the ribbon into position, stitching it 7–8mm (⅜in) from the top of the stocking.

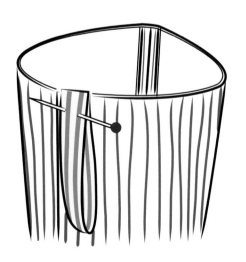

6. Drop the outer stocking inside the lining so that the right sides are together. Pin the top edges together and machine Icm (½in) from the top edge.

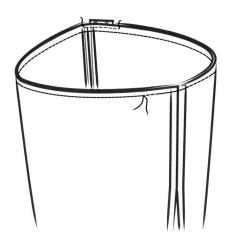

I'd recommend synthetic curtain interlining for this as it is good value and washes well.

7. Trim the seams of the interlining around the top edge as close as possible to the row of machine stitching.

8. Pull the outer stocking through the hole in the back of the lining and slip-stitch the gap to close it. Tuck the lining into the outer stocking. (The loop of ribbon will now appear on top of the finished stocking.

9. Roll the seam on the top edge between your fingers until it is flat, then press with an iron and topstitch.

VARIATIONS

✕ The stocking can be scaled down to make smaller versions for your Christmas tree, which can be filled with treats – a hit with young and old alike.

✕ To personalise the stocking, you could add the letters of the child's name, following the same appliqué techniques and making similar templates to the ones provided for the Doorway Puppet Theatre (pages 282–285).

CRAFTS

SEWING TIDY BAG

This is a really useful bag for holding all the stray bits and pieces that accumulate when you have a sewing project on the go. A pin cushion filled with sterilised sand anchors the bag to a work surface, while parcel strapping inserted in the top gives a rigid edge to ensure the bag stays open for easy access while you're working. Put pins and needles in the pin cushion; use the bag itself for snipped threads and fabric trimmings. It can be used for countless other purposes too – even as somewhere handy to store the TV remote!

YOU WILL NEED

Main fabric: 50cm (20in) square of cotton (or a 'fat quarter' from a patchwork shop) for the outer bag

Lining: 50 x 20cm (20 x 10in) contrasting cotton for lining the outer bag

Scrap fabric: 26 x 13cm (10 x 5in) strip for the inner pin cushion

Thread: All-purpose sewing thread

Accessories: 250g (9oz) sterilised sand (such as children's play sand or aquarium sand from a pet shop)

Im (1⅛yd) parcel strapping Icm (½in) wide (see tip on page 162)

CUTTING OUT

Main fabric
Cut out one 50 x 25cm (20 x 10in) piece for the outer bag; two 20 x 10cm (8 x 4in) strips for the strap; two 13cm (5in) squares for the outer pin cushion.

Lining
Cut out one 50 x 25cm (20 x 10in) piece.

Scrap fabric
Cut out two 13cm (5in) squares for the inner pin cushion.

ASSEMBLY

Outer bag and lining

1. Fold the lining in half lengthways, right sides together, then pin and machine-stitch the side seams, Icm (½in) from the edges, leaving an 8cm (3¼in) gap in the middle of one side. Repeat with the fabric for the outer bag, but this time do not leave a gap in the seam (see diagram overleaf).

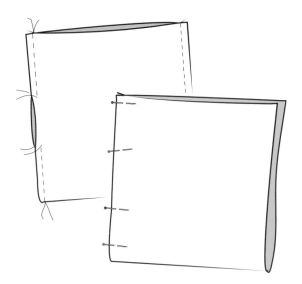

2. Press the bottom edge to give a sharp crease. Press open the side seams of both the lining and the outer bag. Tweak the lining so that one side seam lies directly over the crease in the bottom of the fabric and the corner flattens out into a right-angled triangle. Press and pin. Measure 2.5cm (1in) from the tip of the triangle and draw a line across with tailor's chalk or a water-soluble marker pen. Machine-stitch along the line, then trim off the excess fabric. Do this on all bottom corners of both the lining and outer bags.

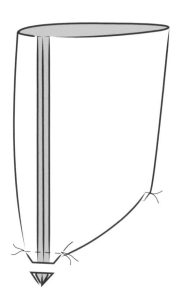

Strap

1. Place the two pieces of fabric for the strap right sides together, then pin and machine along the long sides.

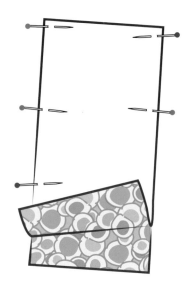

2. Turn the fabric through to the right side, roll the seams right to the edge with your fingers and press.

3. Pin or tack the strap to the centre of one side of the outer bag, with right sides together and the strap hanging down the bag, then machine-stitch it in place.

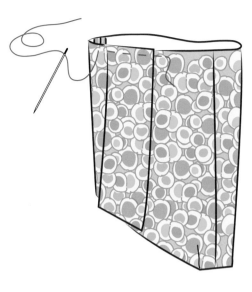

3. Machine-stitch around the top of the bag, 1.5cm (⅝in) from the top, to form a casing for the parcel strapping.

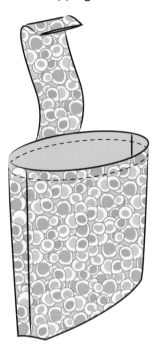

Assembling the bag and pin cushion

1. Place the outer bag inside the lining, with right sides together and the side seams aligned. Pin and machine along the top edge, 1cm (½in) from the edge.

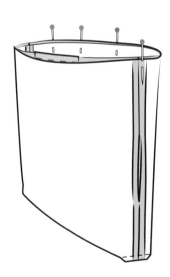

4. Sandwich the two pieces of the outer pin cushion, right sides together, onto the free end of the strap. Machine-stitch along the side and top edges of the pin cushion, making sure you don't catch the strap in the stitching on the sides.

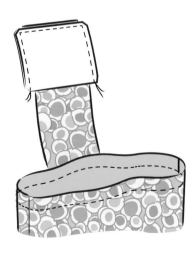

2. Turn the bag through the gap in the lining, then slip-stitch the gap closed and tuck the lining into the outer bag. Press the upper edges.

CRAFTS

5. Trim the corners, then pull the pin cushion right side out so that it protrudes from the end of the strap.

6. Place the pieces of fabric for the inner pin cushion right sides together, then pin and machine around all four edges, leaving a 5cm (2in) gap in the middle of one side. Turn the bag through the gap and fill with sterilised sand. Sew the gap together with small hand stitches.

7. Insert the filled inner pin cushion into the outer pin cushion, fold over the edges and slip-stitch together.

8. To insert the parcel strapping, first unpick a few machine stitches in the lining in the casing seam at the top of the bag.

9. Snip away the sharp edges of one end of the parcel strapping (to prevent snagging) and then carefully feed the strapping into the casing at the top edge of the bag. Overlap the ends inside and slip-stitch the gap shut. Your bag is now ready to go!

Whenever I get a parcel in the post, I save the strapping as it always comes in useful – perfect for using in this bag, for instance. Just make sure that you use a piece without any angles in it (from being wrapped around a parcel) to ensure the bag stays open properly.

Patchwork and quilting shops sell fabric in fat quarters, two of which are ideal for the Pyramid Box or Sewing Tidy.

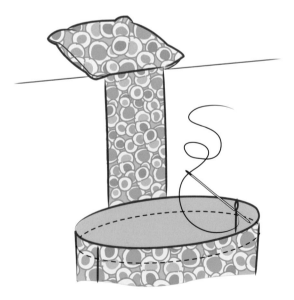

CRAFTS

CRAFTS

PYRAMID BOX

These boxes make super birthday or Christmas presents. I have made many of them over the years, including twelve for a charity a couple of years ago. My mother helped me on this occasion. Despite suffering from early dementia, she found the different stages of the projects straightforward and engrossing, while the joy at finding out how much money we had raised really boosted her self-esteem.

YOU WILL NEED

Templates and box card: Tracing paper
　　Empty cereal packets for the templates
　　and inner box
　　Two A4 pieces of mount board for the
　　outer box
Main fabric: 40 x 115cm (16 x 45in) cotton for the
　　outer box, pin cushion, pocket and needle
　　case
Lining: 40cm (16in) square of cotton for
　　the inner box
Interlining: 20cm (8in) square of felt or
　　interlining for the 'pages' of the needle
　　case booklet
　　50cm (20in) 70g (2oz) wadding, 70cm (27½in)
　　wide
Thread: All-purpose sewing thread
Needle: Fine curved needle for stitching the
　　outer and inner box together
Accessories: Craft knife for cutting the
　　mount board
　　Masking tape
　　Craft hole punch or skewer
　　5 x 12cm (2 x 4½in) piece of pelmet buckram
　　1m (1⅛yd) ribbon or cord 5mm (¼in) wide
　　Good-quality glue stick
　　3 paper fasteners and 3 small brass rings
　　Beads

CUTTING OUT AND ASSEMBLY

Templates and box card

1. Trace the four templates (for the outer and inner boxes, to mark holes for fastenings and for the pin cushion) onto card to make a set of master templates. For the outer and inner boxes, it's important to draw around same template for every piece you're cutting out so that hey're all the same size.

2. Using the templates, mark and cut out all the card pieces needed for the outer and inner boxes: four triangles from mount board for the outer box and four triangles from cereal-packet card for the inner box.

Outer and inner triangles

1. Place the four outer mount board triangles together to form a larger triangle and stick them together with masking tape on one side only (see tip on page 169 and diagram overleaf).

2. On the three points of this larger triangle mark and, with a craft hole punch or skewer, punch holes for the paper fastenings using the template (see diagram overleaf).

3. Place the four cereal-packet card triangles together to form a large triangle to line the box. Leaving a 2mm (⅛in) gap between pieces, tape them together with masking tape, again taping on one side of the large triangle only.

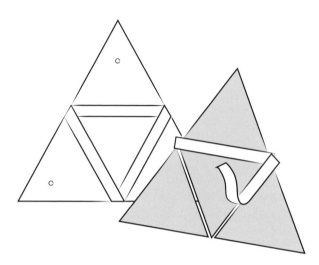

4. Place the outer triangle on the outer fabric and draw around it using a chalk pencil. Cut out the fabric, cutting at least 2.5cm (1in) beyond the drawn line all around.

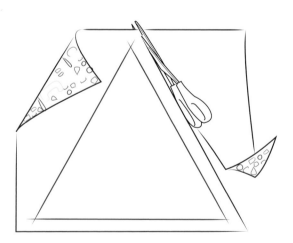

5. Repeat with the inner triangle on the lining fabric.

Pocket

1. Cut out a 10 x 20cm (4 x 8in) strip from the outer fabric to make the pocket.

2. Fold under 5mm (¼in) and then 1cm (⅜in) along both long edges of the pocket and press. Machine-stitch.

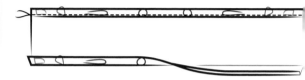

Pin cushion

1. Cut two 13cm (5in) squares from the outer fabric. Cut a 13cm (5in) length of ribbon or cord and fold it in half to make a loop. Tack the raw ends of the loop to one corner of one of the squares, on the right side, so that the loop points diagonally in towards the centre of the square. Place the other outer fabric square right side down on top. Draw around the pin cushion template on the fabric.

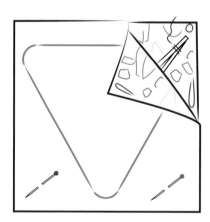

2. Machine-stitch along this line, leaving a 5cm (2in) gap in the middle of one side and making sure you catch the raw ends of the ribbon loop in the stitching. Trim the edges to within 2mm (⅛in) of the stitching.

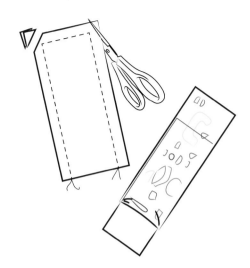

3. Turn the fabric right side out through the opening. Stuff the pin cushion with offcuts of wadding and slip-stitch the gap closed.

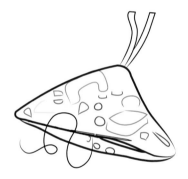

Needle case booklet

1. Cut two 6 x 12cm (2½ x 5in) pieces of outer fabric for the cover of the needle case booklet. Place them right sides together and machine-stitch on three sides, 5mm (¼in) from the edge, leaving one short end open. Trim the corners and turn the fabric right side out through the opening. Press.

2. Insert the piece of pelmet buckram into the cover. Fold under the edges of the opening, press and slip-stitch together.

3. Cut out two strips of felt or interlining to make the 'pages' of the booklet. They should be slightly shorter and narrower than the needle case cover. Position them on the inside of the cover and machine-stitch along the centre to form the spine of the booklet.

Making up the box

1. Use a glue stick to spread glue all over the prepared outer triangle of mount board, on the side without the masking tape. Place the triangle on the wadding, glue side down, and cut out the wadding to exactly the same size as the triangle.

2. Spread glue all over the prepared inner triangle of card, on the side with the masking tape. Place the triangle on the wadding, glue side down, and cut out the wadding to exactly the same size as the triangle.

3. Place the outer triangle, wadding side down, in the middle of the wrong side of the triangle of outer fabric. Fold over and glue down the points of the fabric triangle and then fold over the edges and glue them onto the card.

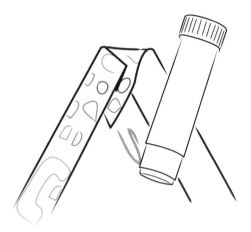

4. Insert a paper fastener and brass ring through each hole in the outer box layer and tape the fastener into position.

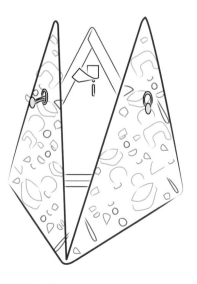

5. Repeat step 3 to glue the inner card triangle onto the lining fabric.

6. Fold up the sides of the inner triangle, so that you know where the pocket needs to go, then slip-stitch the lower edge of the pocket to the base on one edge of the inner pyramid.

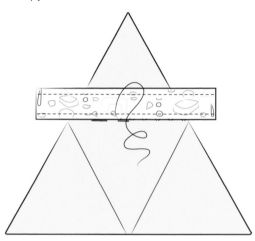

7. Glue the ribbon straps and the edges of the pocket into position.

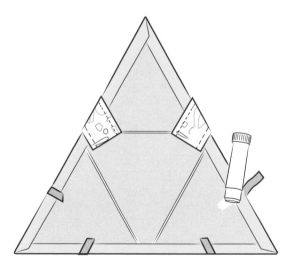

8. Tuck the folded piece of ribbon on the corner of the pin cushion between the two layers of the box in one corner of the base of the box and glue into position.

9. Spread glue on the card side of the inner triangle, then place on the card side of the outer triangle and peg the sections together until they are stuck firmly.

10. Take a fine curved needle and ladder-stitch (see page 51) all edges of both triangles together.

11. Thread the remaining ribbon or cord through the rings on the outside of the box. Knot some beads on to the ends.

12. Pull up the edges of the glued-together triangles using the ribbon, then tie the ends of the ribbon into a bow to hold the box together. Position the pin cushion on the base, anchored by its ribbon. Fold up the needle case booklet and tuck it under the other strap. For the finishing touch, you could insert a few needles in the booklet and some colourful pins in the pin cushion – all ready to go!

VARIATIONS

× The basic design could easily be adapted into a jewellery box or made in a different size as a decorative box for holding a child's toy.

When joining pieces together for the outer and inner boxes, stick masking tape along one side, turn over and butt the second piece up against the first piece.

HOME
FURNISHINGS

HOME FURNISHINGS

CUSHIONS

Cushions are a fabulous addition to any scheme. Fun in a child's bedroom and sophisticated in a living room, they do not take a lot of fabric andd they are a wonderful place to start when you are learning to sew. They can be simple or complex, plain or fancy!

WRAPPED CUSHION COVER

This is the easiest type of cushion cover to make and a good way of starting your sewing journey! It is also a really economical use of fabric, as it's just one strip with no extra bits and pieces to attach. You could use ties to fasten the cover if you'd prefer not to make buttonholes.

MEASURING UP

If you are making this to fit a different-sized cushion pad, you'll need a rectangle of fabric twice the width of the pad plus 30cm (12in) x the width of the pad plus 3cm (1¼in).

YOU WILL NEED

Pad: 45cm (17½in) square cushion pad
Fabric: 48 x 120cm (18 x 47in) furnishing fabric
Thread: All-purpose sewing thread
Accessories: Three 29mm (1⅛in) self-cover
  buttons (see page 112)

ASSEMBLY

1. Neaten all raw edges (see page 82). Turn over 12cm (4½in) to the wrong side on each short end. On one short end, make three 32mm (1¼in) buttonholes (see page 69).

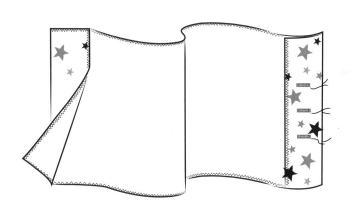

2. Fold the strip of fabric into three, with the right side of the fabric on the inside and the two short edges overlapping in the middle and the edge without the buttonholes on top (see diagram overleaf). The square central section should measure the width of the pad plus 3cm (1¼in).

HOME FURNISHINGS

3. Make sure all edges are parallel, then pin together the top and bottom edges.

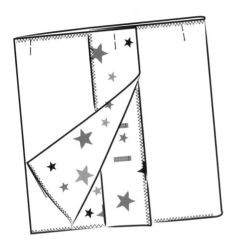

4. Machine-stitch the edges of the cover together, taking 1.5cm (⅝in) seam allowances.

5. Turn the cover right side out and press the seams, pushing out the corners with a chopstick or point turner. Cover the buttons (see page 112) and sew them on.

BOXED CUSHION COVER

Cushion covers of this kind are made to cover box-shaped foam pads, such as you might find on a sofa, for instance, or to go on the seat of a wooden chair, as shown here. They are also really effective with a standard cushion pad popped in. I have put a 50cm (20in) square cushion pad inside my 35cm (13½in) box cover (see photo on page 177) – yes, it really does fill it up nicely!

MEASURING UP

The sample here is 35cm (13½in) square with a box strip 5cm (2in) deep, but you can follow the instructions below to make any size of box-shaped cushion. Simply measure the size of the pad across the top, down the sides and around the perimeter, adding a 1.5cm (⅝in) seam allowance all round and allowing for extra seams in the back section of the strip in which the zip is inserted.

YOU WILL NEED
Pad: 35cm (13½in) foam pad or 50cm (20in) square cushion pad
Fabric: 80cm (31½in) furnishing fabric, 137cm (54in) wide
Thread: All-purpose sewing thread
Machine foot: Adjustable zipper foot (see page 56)
Accessories: 3m (3¼yd) no. 3 piping cord 30cm (12in) zip

CUTTING OUT

Cut the following from the fabric: two 38cm (15in) squares for the front and back of the cover; two 5 x 30cm (2 x 12in) strips for the back section with the zip; one 8 x 118cm (3¼ x 46½in) strip that will form the remainder of the box. (You may need to join two or more strips of fabric together for this.)

ASSEMBLY

1. Neaten the edges of all the cushion cover pieces with zigzag stitching or overlocking, then follow the instructions for the Piped Cushion Cover (page 180) for making and attaching piping, attaching piping to both square panels for this cover.

2. Next, join together the two narrower strips of fabric for the back edge of the cushion, inserting a zip in the centre of the two long edges following the instructions on page 114.

3. Pin one short end of this zipped section to a short end of the long strip, right sides together, then machine-stitch in place. Press the seam open.

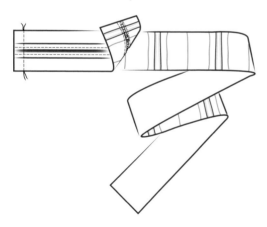

4. To attach the long strip to one of the square pieces of fabric, start with the zipped section, positioning it (right sides together with the square piece) so that the zip sits in the middle of the back of the cushion.

5. Carefully pin your strip to one of the piped square pieces, sandwiching the piping in between the two layers. Continue in this way until you reach the other side of the zipped section.

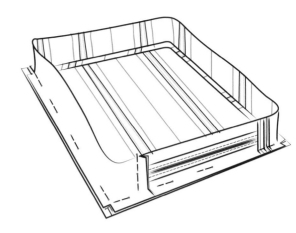

6. Pin and join this short seam so that the square piece is completely enclosed.

7. Now machine the strip to the piped square, following the row of machining that is holding the piping in position. Snip the box strip at each corner to make it easier to position around the edge of the piped square, taking care not to cut into the stitching.

8. Open the zip (so that you can turn the cover through), then pin the second piped square of fabric to the other side of the box strip in the same way, positioning them right sides together and lining up the corners on the top and bottom of the strip. Machine together.

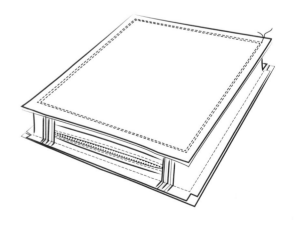

EASY OXFORD COVER

A really classy finish for cushion covers or pillowcases. The traditional way of making an Oxford cover is to add an extra piece of fabric all the way round the edge of the pillowcase or cushion cover, which requires extra cutting out and seam finishing, not to mention fashioning mitred corners. A few months ago, I was looking at a commercially made pillowcase and noticed how the border hadn't been added separately: the extra fabric was incorporated into the width and length of the cover, requiring no insertions, just careful measuring. This is the method that I've gone for here. Have a pillowcase to hand while you make this and all will be revealed. The hardest bit is doing the sums!

MEASURING UP

The cover that I've made fits a 50cm (20in) square cushion pad and has a 3cm (1¼in) border all round, but the instructions below can easily be adapted for any size of pillow or pad. Just measure your pillow or cushion and decide how big you'd like the border to be, then substitute your own measurements, allowing for a 1.5cm (⅝in) seam allowance top and bottom. You will notice that the back cushion section is slightly narrower than the front: this is to avoid the opening being caught in the topstitching for the border at the end.

YOU WILL NEED

Pad: 50cm (20in) square cushion pad
Fabric: 59 x 132cm (23 x 52in) cotton
Thread: All-purpose sewing thread

ASSEMBLY

1. Neaten each short end of the strip of fabric with a double hem: turn over the edge by 1cm (½in), press, and then turn over by 2cm (¾in) and press again. Machine-stitch in place.

2. Find the fold lines by measuring and marking 52cm (20½in) and 108cm (42½in) from one short edge. Fold along the fold lines and pin together along the top and bottom raw edges. The shorter flap should overlap the deeper one.

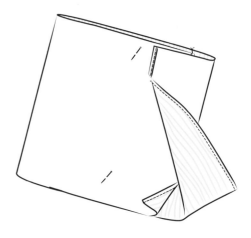

3. Machine-stitch along both raw edges of the cushion cover (see diagram overleaf). There's no need to neaten these seams, as the edges will be enclosed.

HOME FURNISHINGS

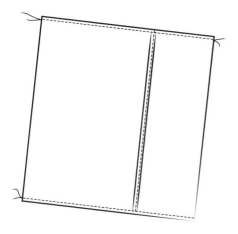

4. Turn the cover right side out and press, pushing the corners out with a point turner or chopstick.

5. Pin just inside the border to secure the back and front of the cushion cover, holding it flat. Now carefully topstitch along every side to create the border, stitching 3cm (1¼in) from the edge. Look at my tips for sewing parallel to an edge (page 67).

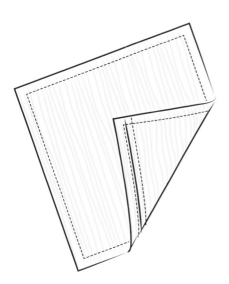

6. Place your cushion or pillow in the finished cover exactly as you would insert a pillow in a pillowcase. And there you have it – a little touch of fabric origami for a fabulous finish!

PIPED CUSHION COVER

Piping gives a really professional finish to a cushion cover and it's actually very straightforward to do. The piping can be made in the same fabric as the cover (as here), or in a contrasting fabric. Piping cord comes in several sizes; no. 3 is a good average thickness and just right for a cushion of this size. It is available in either 100 per cent cotton, which you'll need to wash before using as it shrinks (this also makes it thicken), or in a synthetic material that it does not need to be pre-shrunk. I prefer the latter, as it does not change size or shape.

MEASURING UP

My cover is made to fit a 48cm (18in) cushion pad, but it can of course be made to fit a cushion of any size. You'll need two squares of fabric the same size as your cushion pad, plus a 1.5cm (⅝in) seam allowance on all sides.

YOU WILL NEED

Pad: 48cm (18in) square cushion pad
Fabric: 60cm (24in) furnishing fabric, 152cm (60in) wide
Thread: All-purpose sewing thread
Machine foot: Adjustable zipper foot (see page 56)
Accessories: 2.5m (2¾yd) no. 3 piping cord 36cm (14in) zip

CUTTING OUT

Cut out two 51cm (20in) squares from the fabric. You will have some spare fabric to the side of the two squares that you can use to cut bias strips to cover your piping cord (see page 104). To calculate the width of the strips of fabric, you need enough to cover the cord and give a good 1.5cm (⅝in) seam allowance.

ASSEMBLY

Piping the edge of the cover

1. Cut enough cord to go around the perimeter of the cushion, plus 5cm (2in) extra for the join at each end.

2. Wrap a length of bias binding around the cord with the raw edges of the binding meeting and tack in place, leaving both ends of the binding open by at least 5cm (2in).

3. Using a zipper foot, and taking care not to stitch over the piping, machine-stitch the binding around the cord.

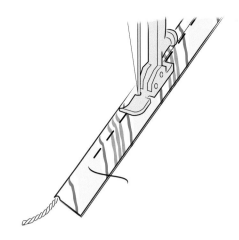

4. Neaten the raw edges of both cushion cover squares with zigzag stitching or overlocking.

5. Position the piping on the right side of one of the pieces of fabric, starting in the middle of one side and with the raw edges of the binding aligning with the edge of the panel. Machine-stitch the piping in place, leaving the ends free either side of the join.

6. Ease the piping around the corners of the panel and clip the seam allowances, if necessary.

7. The traditional way of joining piping cord is to splice the ends together and bind them with thread. When I showed this

method to my students, they begged me to demonstrate a simpler technique – so here it is! Cut one end of the binding at a 45° angle and fold the raw edge under. Lay the other end of the binding inside the fold, overlapping by about 5cm (2in). Cut the ends of the cords so that they meet and then sew the ends together with hand stitching. Wrap the binding around the cord and pin, tack and machine in place.

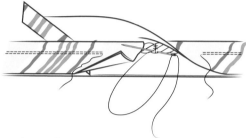

Attaching the zip

1. Place the piped and unpiped cushion cover panels right sides together. Position the zip in the middle of one side of the panels and use pins to mark where the zip starts and finishes. Pin and machine the seam on either side of the zip, leaving the area between the pins unstitched.

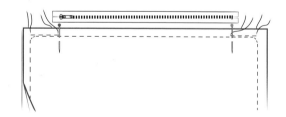

2. Open out the cushion cover pieces, wrong side up, so that you can get to this seam. Open the zip and place one side right side down so that the teeth sit next to the piping. Machine in place close to the teeth, stitching on the seam allowance fabric only.

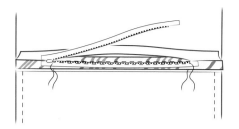

3. Turn the cushion cover pieces right side up and fold under the open seam allowance where you're going to attach the zip. Close the zip, then pin and tack the other side of the zip to the seam allowance, 6mm (¼in) from the folded edge. Machine stitch from the right side, 8mm (⅜in) from the folded edge.

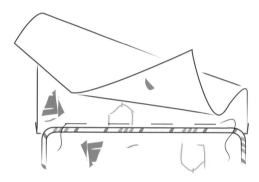

4. Open the zip. (This is important or you won't be able to turn the cushion cover through!) Place the front and back panels of the cushion cover right sides together with the piped panel uppermost. Pin the last three sides of the cushion cover together and machine along the line of stitching holding your piping in place. With this as a guide, it is really easy to sew the seam accurately.

Alternative fastening

If the details of putting the zip in the seam look too tricky or seem like too much effort, you can machine the cover on three sides and simply slip-stitch this side together once you have put your cushion pad in the cover. Just undo the stitches when you need to clean the cover and stitch in place again after cleaning.

HOME FURNISHINGS

HOME FURNISHINGS

ROMAN BLIND

made my first Roman blind over 30 years ago for one of my children's
bedrooms. In those days, no fancy tracks and fittings were available and I used
a simple wooden batten with screw eyes for attaching the blind. This is actually
still one of the best ways of fixing a blind to a window, and certainly a lot cheaper
than any of the alternatives, and it is the method I'll be explaining here.

Roman blinds have really caught on over the
years and look fabulous at any window. They
re economical, too, as they use a very small
quantity of fabric in comparison to curtains.
t makes it possible to invest in a small piece
of expensive fabric that might be beyond
your budget if made into curtains for the
same window. When blinds are down, they
can give the impression of a wall hanging, so
you can really go to town with your choice of
design, although care should be taken on the
positioning of patterns, checks and stripes.
The blind I've made here is made from a single
width of curtain fabric. For a larger window
you might need to join two or more widths of
fabric together. If so, you'll need to match up
any patterns, in the same way as you would for
curtains (see page 193).

MEASURING UP

To work out how much fabric you require, you
need first to decide whether you would like
the blind on the inside of the window recess or
on the outside. The instructions and diagrams
I've included are for a blind placed outside the
window recess.

  Measure the width and length of the
recess; this will give you the minimum overall
size for the finished blind. A blind fixed
outside the window recess could be wider and

longer than the one shown here; there are no
real restrictions here. You will also need to
calculate roughly how many folds (and hence
dowelling rods) will appear in the blind, on the
basis that each rod should be a minimum of
30cm (12in) apart, with a half fold at the bottom.

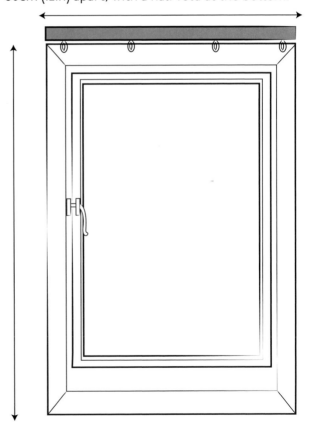

YOU WILL NEED

Main fabric: If your window can be covered by one width of fabric (including an 8cm/3¼in seam allowance for the side hems), then all you need to take into account when buying fabric is the length of the finished blind plus hem allowances top and bottom (see step 1) and 4cm (1½in) for each rod pocket. For a blind with four rod pockets measuring 125cm (49in) when finished, you'd therefore need 153.5cm (61in) of fabric.

Lining: You need exactly the same amount of lining. (Although you make the lining slightly shorter, extra fabric is used up in the rod pockets.)

Thread: All-purpose sewing thread

Accessories: Wooden batten and screw eyes
    Drill and nails for attaching the batten
    1 length of sew-and-stick Velcro, 20mm (¾in) wide
    Staple gun for attaching the Velcro
    Blind rings
    Dowelling rods measuring 1cm (½in) in diameter, each cut to the width of the finished blind
    Weight bar cut to 1cm (½in) narrower than the width of the blind (available in kit form)
    Roman blind cord (each length approximately one and half times the length of the blind plus the width of the blind)
    Blind acorn and cord connector
    Cleat for attaching the cord to the wall

Top Tip

Allow a little extra fabric when purchasing, as the cut edges of the fabric may not be completely straight.

ASSEMBLY

Making the blind and lining

1. With the wrong side of the fabric facing you, turn over 2.5cm (1in) on the top edge, 4cm (1½in) on each side edge, and a double 5cm (2in) hem on the bottom edge. Mitre the top corners and press all edges.

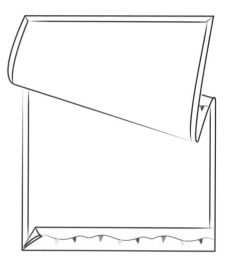

2. With the wrong side of the lining uppermost, turn over each edge at the side by 2.5cm (1in) and press in place. (The lining should be about 1cm/½in narrower than the main fabric on each side – you may need to adjust this before turning over the hems.)

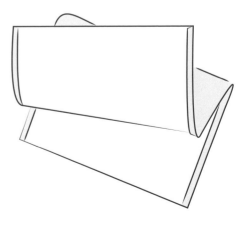

3. Calculate the position of the rod pockets (see 'Measuring Up') and mark the casings for these on the right side of the lining, using a ruler and a chalk pencil or a retractable pencil (top half of diagram below). These should consist of a series of parallel lines 4cm (1¾in) apart, which, when sewn together, will form tucks in the lining.

4. Match up each set of parallel lines drawn on the lining, forming a series of little folds poking up on the right side of the lining. Pin together and machine-stitch in place (bottom half of diagram above). Press the rod pockets towards the hem of the blind.

6. Machine along the folded lower edge of the blind to make a casing at for inserting the weight bar.

Attaching fastenings and hanging the blind

Before hanging your blind, you'll first need to attach the wooden batten to the top of the window recess and staple the adhesive 'hook' side of the piece of Velcro to this. You can attach the cleat for the cord to the wall at this stage too, if you wish, although you may prefer to do this after you've put up the blind, to work out the best position for it. Prepare the blind as follows:

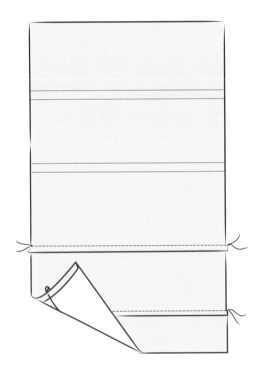

5. Place the lining and main fabric wrong sides together, with the top of the lining close to the top of the main fabric (the raw edge will be hidden by the Velcro). Now attach the main fabric and lining to each other by machining just above the stitching line at the top of each rod pocket.

1. Pin the loop piece of the strip of Velcro to the top of the blind, on the lining side and machine in place, stitching along both edges in the same direction. This prevents the fabric from twisting.

2. Hand-sew blind rings to the edge of each rod pocket, about 2cm (¾in) in from the edge of the blind. Then attach further rings at regular intervals along each pocket (about 30–40cm/12–16in apart), making sure that the rings align above each other in vertical rows; you'll have about four per pocket for a standard-sized blind, as here, more if the blind is wider (see diagram overleaf).

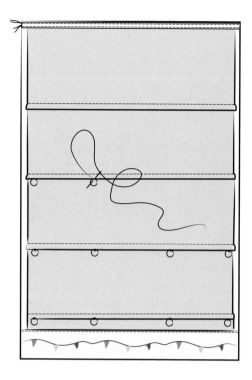

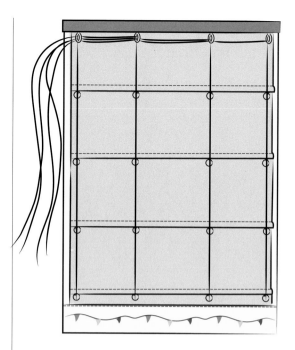

3. Slip-stitch the sides of lining to the sides of the main fabric.

4. Insert the rods and weight bar and hand sew the ends of the casings shut.

5. Attach screw eyes to the batten in line with the blind rings. Thread a length of cord through each of the blind rings, starting by knotting the cord to the ring at the bottom of the blind, then through each ring directly above, running through to the top of the blind.

6. Attach the top of the blind to the Velcro strip on the wooden batten and thread the cords through the screw eyes, feeding all of them through the screw eye furthest to the left. Feed the cords into the cord connector and attach the blind acorn to the end of the cord.

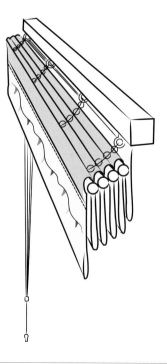

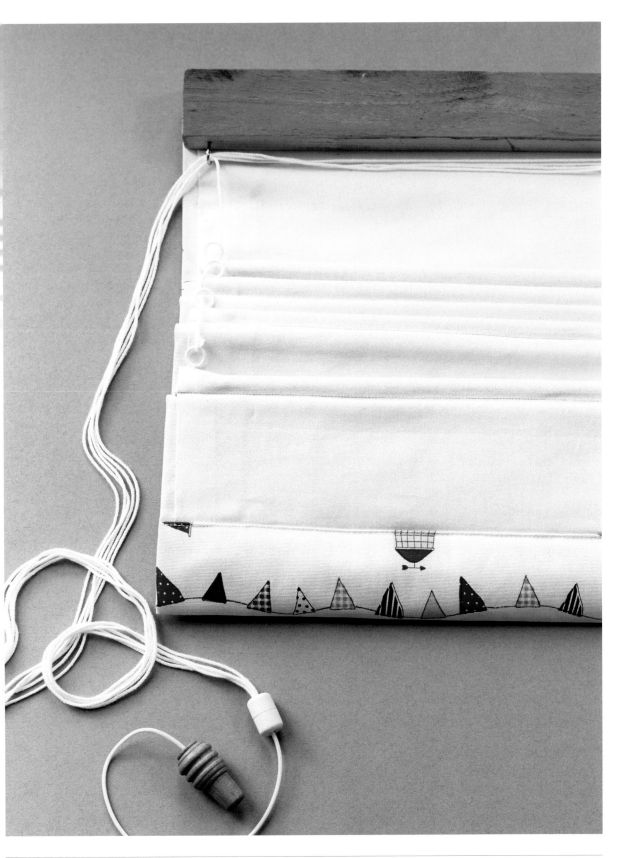

HOME FURNISHINGS

HOME FURNISHINGS

CURTAINS

Making a new set of curtains is the perfect way to refurbish a room at a fraction of the cost of having them made up professionally and with the satisfaction of knowing that yours will be truly unique. There is some maths involved, but the wonderful range of fabrics now available gives you endless scope.

YOU WILL NEED

Main fabric and lining: See the example in the box on page 192

Thread: All-purpose sewing thread (see tip on page 196)

Accessories: Curtain weights (optional Heading tape at 8cm (3in) wide to fit width of each curtain when sewn together and hemmed at the sides

Curtain hooks

MEASURING UP

1. Measure the length of the curtain track or pole (marked 'A' in the diagram).

2. To give you the finished length or 'drop' of the curtain, measure from the track to the sill or the desired point below the window (marked 'B' in the diagram).

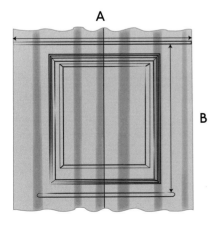

3. To allow enough fullness in the curtains, each one needs to be at least 2–2.5 times as wide as the track before being gathered. This means that you often have to stitch two pieces of fabric together for one curtain to have the required fullness – the curtain thus has two 'drops'.

4. To each 'drop' of fabric you need to add an extra 22cm (9in) for the hems at the top and bottom of the curtain. This is for a standard taped heading; you need to allow 40cm (16in) for a hand-pleated heading.

5. To calculate the length of each drop, you also need to take into account the pattern repeat as it's important that the design matches all the way across both curtains. The size of the pattern repeat will vary depending on the size of the design. A roll of fabric will often have a label on the end giving the size of pattern repeat. If not, you can easily check yourself. Measure from one point on the pattern along the selvedge to exactly the same point on the next pattern.

6. Fold the fabric so that both selvedge edges touch and check that the pattern matches along its length, to make sure that the pattern will flow evenly from one drop to another when they are attached (see diagram overleaf). If it doesn't (which can happen from time to time), it's probably best to avoid buying that particular fabric.

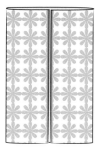

CURTAIN FABRIC CALCULATIONS

Here's how to calculate fabric amounts for a pair of either plain or patterned curtains with a finished length of 148cm (58in), made from three widths of fabric.

MAIN FABRIC: PLAIN

Amount of fabric per curtain drop:
Finished length (148cm/58in) + 22cm (9in) hem allowance = 170cm (67in)

Total amount for one pair of curtains:
170cm (67in) x 3 widths = 510cm (201in)

MAIN FABRIC: PATTERNED

Amount of fabric per curtain drop:
Finished length (148cm/58in) + 22cm (9in) hem allowance = 170cm(67in)

Allow 200cm (80in) for each curtain drop (four complete 50cm (20in) pattern repeats)

Total amount for one pair of curtains made with fabric with a 50cm (20in) pattern repeat:
200cm (79in) x 3 widths = 600cm (237in)

Inevitably there will be some wastage per drop (see diagram, right):
200cm – 170cm = 30cm (79in – 67in = 12in)

LINING

Amount of lining fabric per curtain drop:
Finished length (148cm/58in) + 18cm (7in) hem allowance = 166cm (65in)

Total amount of lining made from three widths of plain fabric:
166cm (65in) x 3 widths = 498cm (195in)

7. To calculate how much fabric you'll need overall, see the example in the box.

FABRIC PREPARATION

If your fabric is creased from being folded up, first press it with an iron.

JOINING DROPS AND PATTERN MATCHING

1. Mark the top of each drop with two crossed pins inserted in one corner of the fabric. Measure out the number of drops you need.

2. When cutting out fabric with a pattern, cut at the bottom of the last complete pattern repeat, as shown in the diagram below, before cutting off the waste fabric. (The offcuts can be made into cushions or valances, so they are not wasted!)

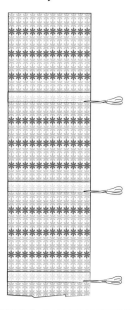

3. To make two curtains from three drops (as in the example in the box), you'll need to cut one drop in half. (Each curtain will consist of one and a half drops.) Fold one drop in half lengthways, selvedge to selvedge, and cut along the fold.

4. Now you need to join these one and a half drops together to create the right width for each curtain. With the right side of the fabric uppermost, fold under the selvedge edge of the full drop and lay it on top of the half drop near the selvedge edge, matching the pattern together exactly. Pin together.

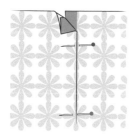

5. To ensure the patterned pieces remain aligned, it's best to tack them together too. Stitch by hand on the right side of the fabric. Fasten the thread at the bottom of seam and slide the needle into the folded edge of the top piece of fabric. Take a small stitch from the bottom piece of fabric and continue along the seam like this.

6. Remove the pins and turn the fabric the wrong side out to reveal a series of long and short tacking stitches.

7. Machine along the row of tacking, then remove the tacking and press the seam open.

ASSEMBLY

Now that you've joined the drops together, you can make up the curtains. For clarity, I've shown these stages with plain fabric, but the principle is exactly the same for a patterned fabric.

Hemming the curtains

1. Fold over the side hems of the main fabric by about 5cm (2in) on to the wrong side of the fabric, pin and press in place. (Any raw edges can first be neatened with zigzag stitching.)

2. Fold over the top hem by 4cm (1½in) (when applying heading tape it is not necessary to have a huge hem) and the bottom one by 8cm (3¼in) and then by 10cm (4in). Press in place.

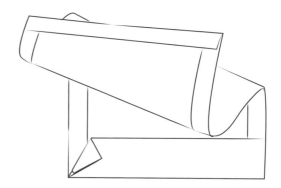

3. Before you stitch the hems, first make a mitre at the lower corner of each curtain where the hem at the side meets the one at the bottom (see box, right). You can, if you wish, stitch a curtain weight covered in lining fabric (see page 195 and step 2 in box) into the corner of the hem while you're folding the mitre.

4. Having folded the mitre, stitch the hems, using catch stich for the hems at the side, slip stitch for the one at the bottom and ladder stitch to catch the folds of the mitre together. The stitches should be worked loosely, without too much tension, so that they do not puncture and pull through to the other side of the fabric.

Lining

When using more than one width of lining (as in the example), machine the selvedge edges together and press open the seams, as for the main fabric.

1. Fold over the fabric at the bottom edge by 8cm (3¼in) and then 10cm (4in), press and machine along the edge of the hem.

2. Fold over the side hems so that they are about 2.5cm (1in) narrower on each side than the completed curtain. (Having assembled the main fabric for the curtains, you may need to adjust the lining to fit before hemming it.) Press in place.

Joining the lining to the curtains

1. Place the lining and curtain wrong sides together, matching the seams, and pin in place, with the lining positioned about 2.5cm (1in) away from the side and bottom edges of the curtain. The top of the lining should be a similar distance from the top of the curtain – the raw edge will be hidden by the heading tape.

MAKING A MITRE

This is how to fold an asymmetrical mitre suitable for hems at the bottom of curtains. For other types of mitre, see page 90.

1. Position a pin at the corner of the bottom hem (pin A) and at the top where it meets the side hem (pin B).

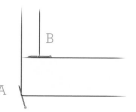

2. Open out the hems and create a diagonal fold from the pin on the side hem across the pin at the corner of the hem, then pin and tack this fold into position.

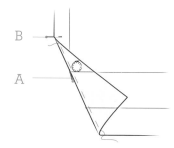

3. Refold the side hem and then the bottom hem, then hand-stitch the side and bottom hems, using ladder stitch to close up the mitre.

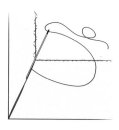

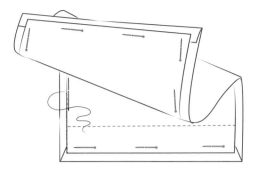

2. Slip-stitch the lining to the curtain.

Attaching the heading tape

1. Place the heading tape along the top of the lined curtain (on the wrong side) close to the side and top edges, folding in the ends of the tape by 3cm (1¼in), and pin in position.

2. At one end of the curtain (the side that will be in the centre of the window) pull the cords to the back of the tape, about 5cm (2in) from the end of the curtain, and tie together securely. Release the cords at the other end of the curtain.

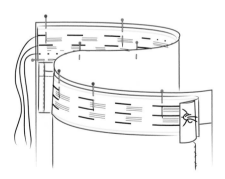

3. If you wish, make a cord tidy bag (one for each curtain – see right) for suspending from the tape to hold the cords when they are pulled to gather up the curtain. This can be sewn in with the heading tape .

4. Machine the tape in place along all edges, making sure to sew each long side in the same direction so that the fabric under the heading tape doesn't twist. Take care not to sew over the cords as you're machining or they won't gather up properly.

Covering a curtain weight (optional)

1. Cut out an 8cm x 5cm (3¼ x 2in) strip from an offcut of curtain lining and fold in half over a curtain weight.

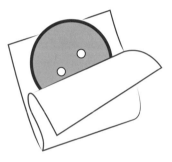

2. Work a row of running stitches around the weight and trim the edges of the fabric, then stitch in place in the hem of the curtain (see step 2 in box, opposite).

Cord tidy bag (optional)

1. Cut out a 20cm x 10cm (8in x 4in) strip from an offcut of curtain lining and machine a 1.5m (⅝in) hem on one short end.

2. Fold the fabric up (with the hem facing in) by 8cm (3¼in) to make a pocket for the cords.

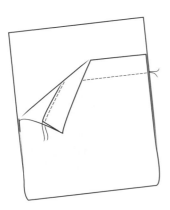

3. Fold in the long edges on either side, enclosing the pocket, and machine a narrow (1.5cm/⅝in) hem on each side.

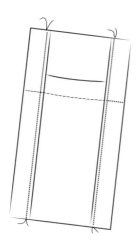

Hanging the curtains

1. Pull the free cords at one end of the curtain to gather it up until it is the desired width, then go across the top of the curtain making sure the gathers are evenly distributed across it. Secure the ends with a slip knot (so that you can release them easily for cleaning the curtains!) and tuck the ends of the cords into the cord tidy bags (if using).

2. Add curtain hooks – inserting one hook roughly every four pockets in the heading tape – and suspend from the curtain rail or pole at the window.

Top Tips

Put your window measurements in a notebook in your bag so that you can consult them at any time. Over the years I have bought fabric in many different places – even on holiday!

You'll find a big reel of cream thread blends well with many different kinds of curtain fabric – you don't need to buy lots of different-coloured thread.

If you're making curtains using plain fabric, you don't need to worry about a pattern repeat, of course. But you do need to ensure that the fabric in each drop is the same way up, especially fabrics with a nap, such as velvet, which look different when hung the other way up.

"TO DRESS CURTAINS
AT THE WINDOW,
arrange fabric in folds,
pin a piece of fabric round them,
& leave
for a couple
of days."

ACCESSORIES

SNOOD

I started making snoods 25 years ago. It was a really cold winter and I made them for the children in our close to wear while tobogganing in the snow! Each one takes only about an hour to make and they are perfect for keeping you cosy in the winter – whether it's snowy or not. The one I've made here is lined with cotton jersey, as I just love the feel of the cotton against my skin. The extra layer has the advantage of making it extra snug, too!

YOU WILL NEED

Main fabric: 50 x 64cm (20 x 25in) fleece fabric
Lining: 30 x 64cm (12 x 24in) cotton jersey in a
   contrasting colour
Thread: Polyester sewing thread
Needle: Ballpoint machine needle size 80/12
   for sewing cotton jersey

CUTTING OUT

See the section on cutting out cotton jersey in Jersey T-shirt, page 248.

ASSEMBLY

For tips on sewing cotton jersey, see the section in Jersey T-shirt, page 248.

1. Fold the fleece in half lengthways, with right sides together. Pin together, then machine stitch along the long raw edge, stitching 1cm (½in) from the edge of the fabric, using a small zigzag stitch (about 1mm/¹⁄₁₆in long and 1mm/¹⁄₁₆in wide); alternatively, use an overlocker to join the seams.

2. Repeat for the jersey lining.

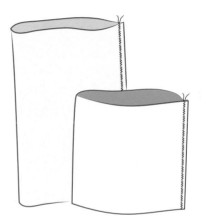

3. Turn the fleece tube right side out. Place the fleece tube inside the jersey tube, so that they are right sides together, aligning the seams. Pin together and machine stitch around the top edge, stitching 1cm (½in) from the top edge.

4. Turn the tube wrong side out and neaten the edges of both jersey and fleece by turning under a Icm (⅜in) hem to the wrong side; you can use a decorative stitch or a small zigzag stitch if you wish.

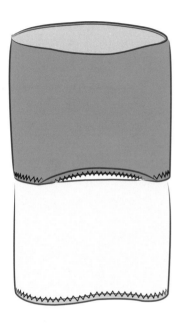

5. Now push the jersey tube all the way down inside the fleece tube, with wrong sides together, until both hems are level and you have a double layer of fabric.

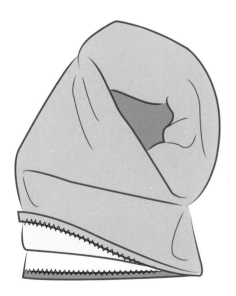

6. This snood can be worn either with the fleece or jersey side on the outside.

VARIATION

× The snood can be made in one long piece of cotton jersey instead to make a lighter-weight garment that can be worn to keep your hair in place on a windy day.

CUT TO EXACT SIZE

8/10

"TAKE TWO

contrasting colour T-shirts

AND CUT UP

to make a

two-tone snood

IN COTTON JERSEY."

1

2

ACCESSORIES

MAN'S APRON

This is a really fun present to make for friends or family members. Indeed, you could kit out the entire family, as one of my students did one Christmas. Setting a budget of £3 per person, she bought a set of curtains from a charity shop and we cut them up, making several fab aprons from the fabric. Adjust the measurements to fit the person you're making it for. Who knows – it may even inspire someone else to have a go at doing the cooking!

YOU WILL NEED

Main fabric: 1.25m (1⅜yd) cotton, at least 115cm (45in) wide, for the apron, ties and neck band
One 7 x 30cm (2¾ x 12in) strip for the pocket (optional)
Contrast fabric: Two 20 x 30cm (8 x 12in) strips of cotton for the pocket
Thread: All-purpose sewing thread
Accessories: Flexible curve ruler for measuring/marking the sides of the apron (optional)

CUTTING OUT

Main fabric

1. Fold the fabric in half lengthways with the selvedges together. Pin the layers together. Using a chalk pencil, mark out the main section of the apron, using the measurements given inthe diagram on the right. This section is positioned along the fold; use a flexible curve ruler to draw the curve from the top of the apron to the side. Cut out.

2. Next mark out the ties, following the measurements in the diagram. Measure a little way in from the selvedge, as this can often be white and therefore show up in the finished apron. Cut out.

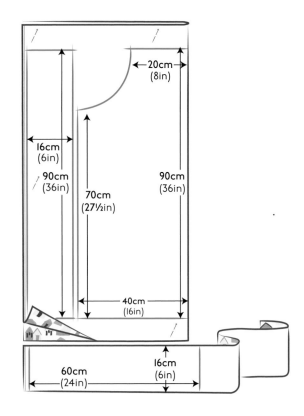

3. Open out the fabric so that you have a single layer, then mark out the neck band along one long edge, again away from the selvedge. Cut out.

ASSEMBLY

Hemming the apron edges

1. With the wrong side of the fabric uppermost, fold over one of the curved edges by 1cm (½in), pressing as you go.

2. Fold over the fabric by another 1cm (½in) and press in place. You will need to stretch as you iron to coax the hem to lie flat. Machine-stitch along the inside edge of the turning.

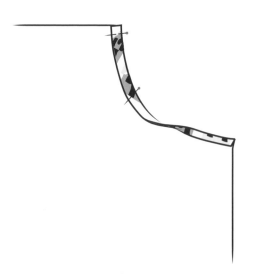

3. Repeat steps 1 and 2 to hem the other curved edge of the apron.

4. To hem each straight edge of the apron (the two sides and top and bottom, turn over each edge by 1cm (½in) and press in place, then turn over by 2cm (¾n) and press again. Machine along the inside edge of each turning. You're now ready to assemble the ties and neck band.

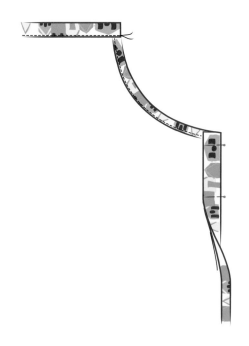

Ties and neck band

I like to make these double thickness so that they are as strong as possible.

1. Fold each tie piece in half lengthways, with wrong sides together, and press to make a crease along the centre of the strap.

2. Open out the strip. Fold under 1cm (½in) on each short end, then fold the two long edges of the fabric in so that they meet at the centre crease.

3. Fold the fabric along the centre crease again, press and pin in place, and topstitch along all four edges.

Pressing curved edges can be tricky. Use a steam iron to help shape the curve.

4. Pin each tie in place at the waist and secure with a square of topstitching. Repeat steps 1–4 to make the neck band and attach in the same way to each top corner of the bib.

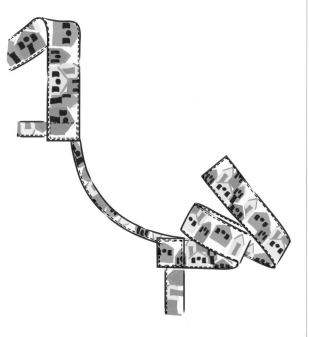

Pocket

Follow the instructions on page 264 for making up the double-patch pocket. You can also add an extra strip of the main fabric for contrast across the front of the pocket (see photo on page 204), if you wish.

ACCESSORIES

CHILD'S SMOCK APRON

Ellie Mae K154

The perfect cover-up for messy activities, the pattern I've used here can be made to fit a child from four to eight years of age; for older children, you could make a smaller version of the Man's Apron on page 204. To make the apron completely waterproof, use a plastic-coated fabric (see tip on page 211).

YOU WILL NEED

Template: Tracing paper
  Empty cereal packet
Main fabric: 1m (1⅛yd) cotton, 115cm
  (45in) wide
Contrast fabric: 50cm (20in) cotton,
  115cm (45in) wide, for the cloud pocket and
  bias binding (to make your own binding, see
  also page 104)
Thread: All-purpose sewing thread
Accessories: 4cm (1¾in) square of paper-
  backed fusible web
  2.5cm (1in) square of Velcro

ASSEMBLY

Follow the pattern for assembling the smock and joining the pieces of bias binding. As instructed in the pattern, fold the binding in half lengthways and press with an iron. For attaching the binding to the smock, I've included a few tips you might like to follow for a better-looking finish – see page 210. I've also included instructions for making a cloud pocket as a simple alternative to the appliqué designs given in the pattern.

Cloud pocket

It is really lovely making shaped pockets. I've provided instructions here for making a cloud-shaped one, but you could make pretty much any compact sort of shape you like.

1. Cut out and pin two pieces of contrast fabric right sides together. These should be slightly larger than your finished pocket shape.

2. Trace the cloud template on page 298 onto cereal-packet card and cut out. Place the template on the fabric and draw round it using a chalk pencil. Machine-stitch along

the drawn line, then cut out the shape, cutting 3mm (1/8in) from the stitching.

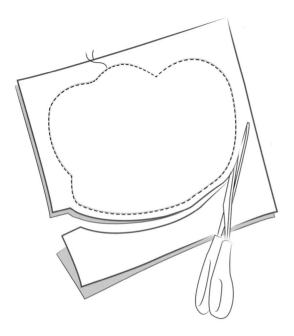

3. Snip into the sharp V-shaped angles on the curves (see page 84). Snip a small cross in what will be the lining of the pocket, taking care to snip through only the top layer of the fabric.

4. Turn the pocket right side out via the small cut and use a chopstick or point turner to push the edges out. Press.

5. Place the fusible web glue side (rough side) down on the wrong side of a scrap of the

contrast fabric and press in place with a steam iron (see page 116).

6. Cut around the web-backed square of fabric and peel off the paper backing. Place the square glue side down over the cut in the cloud pocket and press with the steam iron. This will cover the hole neatly.

7. Position the pocket on the smock, then pin and topstitch (see page 64) into position, remembering to leave the top edge of the pocket open.

Binding

In the pattern it is suggested that you put the binding on the wrong side of the apron and turn to the right side for stitching. This requires very accurate sewing, however, so I suggest you try this instead:

1. Fold the binding in half lengthways, with wrong sides together, and press. Pin the binding to the right side of the smock and stitch in place 1cm (1/2in) from the edge of the garment.

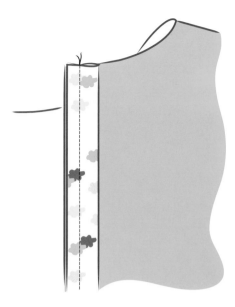

I found this wonderful product called Lamifix in my local patchwork and quilting shop. I was so excited when I was introduced to it. You iron it on to the right side of any fabric and it gives it a plastic coating – how cool is that! I ironed it on to the fabric of one of my aprons, making it wipeable. It means that you can choose any design of fabric you like for the apron rather than being restricted to a smaller range of plastic-coated fabrics. The coating system would also be perfect for making a waterproof bag.

2. Turn the binding over to the wrong side of the smock and pin and tack it in place. Stitching from the right side of the apron just under your first line of stitching, stitch the binding in position; this is called 'stitching in the ditch'. The stitching on the right side of the garment holds the binding in place on the wrong side.

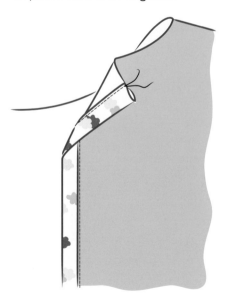

3. Finish by stitching the Velcro in place (for fastening the smock), following the instructions in the pattern.

ACCESSORIES

CAPE
Butterick B4266

I made this beautiful cape several years ago for a friend's daughter to wear on her wedding day. Sadly the pattern I used has been discontinued, but I managed to find a similar pattern, Butterick B4266, which is slightly smaller; you could, of course, make it longer if you wished. The cape shown here is in crushed silk, but you could use a different weight of fabric – a heavy wool for winter wear, for example. The shape is simple and only needs to be fitted at the shoulders. The area that can be a challenge, however, is the very long curved hem. Below I've given a technique for dealing with this beautifully and invisibly.

YOU WILL NEED

(see the pattern for exact fabric requirements)
Fabric: 2.4–2.9m (2⅝–3⅛yd) silk or wool, 115cm (45in) wide, or 1.9–2.3m (2–2½yd) silk or wool, 150cm (60in) wide
Binding: Bias binding, 12mm (½in) wide (to make your own, see page 104)
Thread: All-purpose sewing thread
Accessories: Four 16mm (⅝in) buttons 40–60cm (⅜–⅝yd) 3mm (⅛in) cording

ASSEMBLY

Making a curved hem

Hems are the finishing touch to a garment and usually the last thing you do. Always give yourself time to do a great job and don't be tempted to make too deep a hem here – allow 2.5cm (1in) maximum when turning such a dramatic curve.

1. First, neaten the edge of the hem using zigzag stitches.

2. Fold up the hem and pin in position, then tack close to the folded edge. Tack another line of stitching 2cm (¾in) away from the folded edge, carefully distributing the fullness of the turned-over fabric evenly to create a smoothly curving hem.

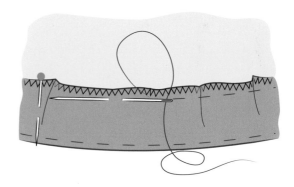

3. Blind-stitch the hem (see page 86).

4. Press lightly on the wrong side of the hem, then remove the tacking. Press again after removing the tacking, making sure that you take the iron just up to the zigzagged edge of the hem but not over it. This hem will be invisible on the right side of the garment.

Shrinking a woollen hem into shape

If you're making a cape out of wool, it's possible to shrink the hem into shape, using a steam iron and applying a bit of pressure.

1. Tack the hem near the folded edge.

2. Run a gathering or easing stitch by hand along the top of the hem (without neatening it first) and pull up in sections so that the hem lies flat.

3. Place a piece of thin card under the hem between the cape and the hem – this will prevent shrinkage of the actual garment!

4. Using a damp pressing muslin or piece of fine cotton (such as a handkerchief) and an iron set to 'wool', apply pressure and heat on the wrong side of the cape. The fullness in the hem will gradually disappear.

5. Neaten the edge of the hem and blind-stitch (see page 86) into position, then remove the tacking and lightly press.

Rouleau button loops

Rather than just plain cording for the button loops (as suggested in the pattern), you could make loops covered in the same fabric as the cape – so long as you're using a lighter weight of fabric, such as silk. Follow the instructions on page 111 to make a reinforced rouleau 60cm (24in) long. Cut it into four equal pieces and attach to the cape, following the instructions in the pattern.

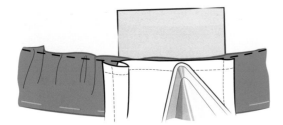

ACCESSORIES

ACCESSORIES

No.5

BUCKET BAG

This is a great bag for taking on holiday to carry all the extra bits and pieces you might need. You could make it in fabric to match your wardrobe, or make more than one to go with different outfits. By choosing a lining that coordinates with the outer fabric and playing around with different variations for the handles and optional pockets, you'll have a bag that's entirely reversible, too.

YOU WILL NEED

Pattern: Gridded paper for scaling up the pattern on page 300

Main fabric: 50cm (20in) cotton, 115cm (45in) wide

Contrast fabric: 50cm (20in) contrasting cotton, 115cm (45in) wide, for the lining

Interlining: 50 x 137cm (20 x 54in) synthetic interlining or 50 x 90cm (20 x 36in) interfacing (see tip on page 219)

Thread: All-purpose sewing thread

CUTTING OUT

Main bag: Using pattern piece A, cut out two pieces each from the main fabric, contrast fabric and interlining. Use a chalk pencil to mark the dots for the handles on the right side of the main fabric.

Base: Using pattern piece B, cut out one piece each from the main fabric, lining and interlining, marking the base dots with tailor's tacks (see page 42) on the right side of main fabric.

Handles: Cut two 7 x 55cm (2¾in x 21½in) strips from the main fabric, two 5 x 55cm (2 x 21½in) strips from the contrast fabric, and two 3.5 x 55cm (1⅜ x 21½in) strips from the interlining.

ASSEMBLY

After machining the sections together, trim the interlining back to the machine stitching on the seams. Press seams with an iron as you work.

Main bag

1. Matching notches together, pin the interlining to the wrong side of the main-fabric bag and base pieces. Replace the paper patterns. Work tailor's tacks (see page 42) at the points marked on the patterns with dots.

2. Place the two main bag pieces right sides together, then pin and machine-stitch the side seams 1cm (½in) from the edge to form a tube. Press the seams open.

3. With right sides together, match the notches on the base (right side uppermost) with those on the main bag and the tailor's tacks on the base to the side seams. Pin and stitch the base to the main bag (see diagram overleaf), then turn the bag right side out ready to add the handles.

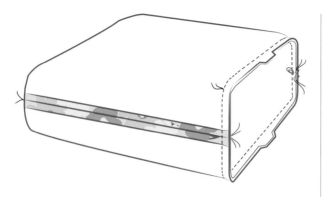

Topstitch along each long edge of the contrast fabric strips.

Handles

1. Fold each main and contrast fabric strip for the handles in half lengthways, with wrong sides together, and press lightly to form a central crease. Open the strips out, then fold the long edges in so that they meet at the centre crease and press again. Slip a strip of interlining under the folded edges of each main fabric strip.

2. Pin a contrast fabric strip over each main fabric strip, aligning the centre creases.

4. On the outside of the bag, position the handles over the marked dots so that they hang down and the raw edges are in line with the top edge of the bag. Pin and machine into place 1cm (½in) from the edge.

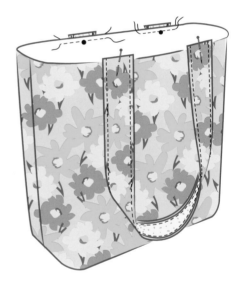

Lining

1. Place the contrast pieces for the lining right sides together, then pin and machine the side seams, leaving a 10cm (4in) gap in the middle of one side.

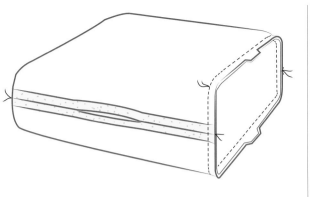

3. Turn the bag right side out through the gap in the lining.

4. Slipstitch (see page 51) the gap in the lining closed, then push the lining down into the outer bag, wrong sides together, taking care to align the side seams.

5. Press the top edge of the bag and topstitch all around, stitching 1.5cm (⅝in) down from the top edge.

VARIATIONS

✗ You can add pockets with a contrast edge to the inside of the bag (see page 259), as I've done for mine, using pieces of the outer fabric for contrast. Make and attach them to the lining before joining the side seams.

✗ You can also add a decorative tie to the outer bag – mine is made using a piece of contrast fabric measuring 10 x 106cm (4 x 42in). Fold the strip in half lengthways, right sides together, then machine-stitch 1cm (½in) from the edge on the three open sides, leaving a 5cm (2in) gap in the middle of the long seam. Turn right side out, then slipstitch the gap closed. The tie is held in place with machine stitching on the side seams of the bag and buttons at intervals (three on each side of the bag) and tied at the front.

2. Attach the lining base as in step 3 of assembling the main bag, but leave the lining wrong side out.

Completion

1. Place the outer bag (right side out) inside the lining bag (wrong side out), so that they are right sides together, with the handles hanging down between the outer and inner layers and with the seams and edges all aligned. Pin and tack together around the top edge.

Interfacing will make your bag slightly stiffer while interlining creates a softer effect. I used curtain interlining for my bag as it washes well.

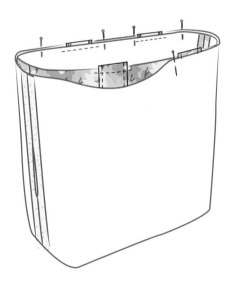

2. Machine-stitch around the top edge of the bag 1cm (½in) from the raw edges.

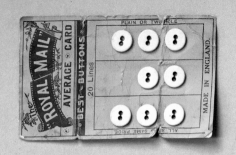

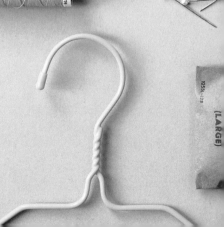

ADULTS' FASHION

ADULTS' FASHION

SHELL BLOUSE
McCall's M2818

This is a lovely wardrobe staple, made in a style with the panels at the side that is known as a 'princess line' – a flattering shape on most figures. My blouse is made in cotton for day wear but you could use other lightweight fabrics. One of my students used this pattern to make a couple of silk blouses to wear in the evening on a cruise!

YOU WILL NEED
(see the pattern for exact fabric requirements)
Fabric: 1.3–1.5m (1½–1⅝yd) cotton or silk, 115cm (45in) wide or 1.1–1.3m (1¼–1⅜yd) cotton or silk, 150cm (60in) wide
Interfacing: 1.3m (1⅜yd) fusible interfacing, 90cm (36in) wide
Thread: All-purpose sewing thread
Accessories: Five 16mm (⅝in) buttons

ASSEMBLY

Fitting panels

My students sometimes have a real problem fitting two curved panels together, so I've offered a few tips here. The way you pin sections together really helps you control your pieces of fabric, ensuring a smooth seam when you sew them together.

1. The front part of the garment has a middle section and two side panels.

2. With right sides together, pin one side panel to the middle section, from the hem of the garment to the first notch.

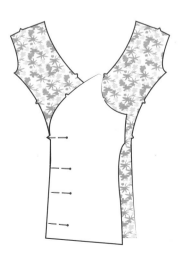

4. Next comes the tricky bit: use your hands to help you – they are the best tool you have! Working with the rounded side section facing you, feed the fabric over your cupped fingers, so that it is pushed upwards in a convex curve, draping over your hand on either side, and pin together. Start from the middle of this section, pinning first in one direction and then in the other. To ease the fullness of the upper fabric into the section below, you pick up little bits of fabric on top and pin them to the section beneath, creating little bubbles of fabric between each pin. On the right side of the garment the finished seam will appear smooth.

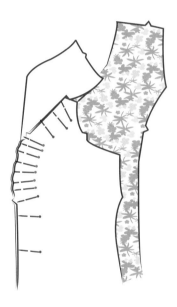

3. Next pin from the armhole to the other notch, leaving the section between the notches unpinned.

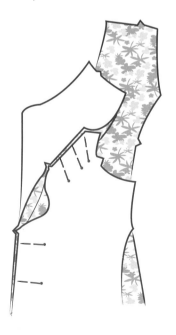

5. Tack and machine the two pieces together. Press the seam open using a tailor's ham or a rolled-up towel (see page 22). Trim the seam to 1cm (½in) and neaten the edges (see page 82).

6. Attach the other panel in the same way, then continue to make the blouse following the instructions supplied with the pattern.

ADULTS' FASHION

ADULTS' FASHION

No.2

SHIFT DRESS
McCall's M6355

This is a really classic style that is simple to make and suitable for any time of year. You can mix and match the different parts of the pattern too – I've combined longer sleeves from one of the tops with the basic shift dress. The pattern can be made in cotton jersey with bust darts only and without a zip – you just slip it over your head. Double-pointed vertical darts can be added for better shaping (see page 91), especially if you're using a non-stretchy fabric, as I've done for this project.

The dress has a zip inserted invisibly in the side seam. I have given you larger diagrams to help you on your way and hopefully make insertion clearer. It is a good idea to stabilise the seam edges prior to inserting the zip, as suggested in the pattern. On my dress I used a narrow fusible stay tape. This prevents the curve of the seam from stretching out of shape.

YOU WILL NEED
(see the pattern for exact fabric requirements)
Fabric: 1.5–2.7m (1⅝–2⅞yd) cotton or cotton jersey, 115cm (45in) wide, plus an extra 0.25m (¼yd) if making long sleeves or 1.3–1.6m (1⅜–1¾yd) cotton or cotton jersey, 150cm (60in) wide, plus an extra 0.25m (¼yd) if making long sleeves
Thread: All-purpose sewing thread
Machine foot: Invisible zip foot
Accessories: Fusible stay tape, 13mm (½in) wide (optional)
   35cm (14in) invisible zip

ASSEMBLY

Concealed zip

This method of inserting a zip is so neat: when the zip is closed, all you see is a line in the seam with a tiny zip pull at the top. Unlike other types of zip insertion, the seam is joined after the zip is inserted. Sewing-machine manufacturers supply a special foot for inserting an invisible zip. As it is not supplied as standard with your sewing machine, you may need to purchase it as an extra.

1. The coils of an invisible zip curl towards the back when the zip is closed – helping to make it less visible than an ordinary zip. To make it easier to sew, it's a good idea to release the tightness of the coils first. Open the zip and, with your iron set to synthetic, press just under the teeth of each coil with the tip of the iron. This enables the zip coil to glide more easily through the grooves in the foot.

2. Before attaching the zip, neaten the raw edges of the seam allowances where the zip is to be inserted (see page 82). Place the open zip face down on the right side of the first piece of fabric with the coil on one side of the zip positioned along the seam line, then pin and tack in place.

3. Fit the right-hand groove of the machine foot over the coil, then stitch this side of the zip in place.

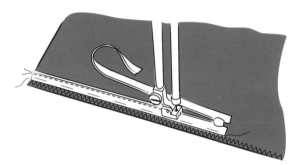

4. Pin and tack the other side of the zip in position, face side down on the right side of the second piece of fabric, with the coil lying along the seam line.

5. Position the left-hand groove of the foot over the coil and stitch the zip into position.

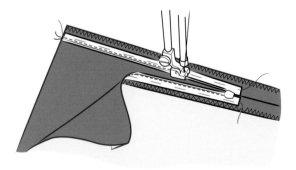

6. Close the zip and change the foot for an ordinary zipper foot. Pin and tack the seam below the zip.

7. Carefully lower the needle into the fabric slightly above and to the left of the machining securing the end of your zip. Machine the rest of the seam from this point, then press open.

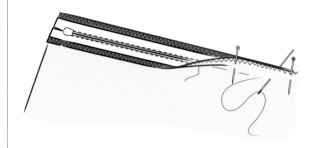

Top Tip

An invisible zip foot is a good investment for a professional finish.

ADULTS' FASHION

ADULTS' FASHION

PENCIL SKIRT
Butterick B5466

In the 1960s I would make mini skirts out of a mere half-metre of fabric – I had about 15 of them. They were so miniscule, I now wince at the thought of me climbing the stairs to sit on top of a London double-decker bus! This skirt is somewhat less revealing but has the advantage of suiting a wider range of ages and sizes. It's hugely versatile, too, as it can be made in almost any fabric you like – wool, cotton or silk – depending on the occasion and time of year.

This skirt also presents a great opportunity to practise various techniques, including zip insertion and making a lining – both outlined below. I will also show you how to make a really easy narrow waistband that stiffens itself and holds its shape.

YOU WILL NEED

(see the pattern for exact fabric requirements)
Fabric: 0.8–1.4m (⅞–1½yd) wool, cotton or silk,
    115cm (45in) wide, or 0.8 (⅞yd) wool,
cotton or silk, 150cm (60in) wide
Lining (optional): 0.8m (⅞yd) polyester or
    acetate, 150cm (60in) wide
Thread: All-purpose sewing thread
Accessories: 18cm (7in) zip
    Narrow masking tape (optional)
    Hook and bar

CUTTING OUT

Lining

If including lining (see page 233), lay the paper pattern that you used for skirt on to the lining fabric and follow the same cutting plan (no need to cut out a waistband).

Waistband

If you are using the self-stiffening waistband suggested on page 233, cut a strip of fabric 11cm (4⅓in) wide (almost twice the width of the band supplied in the pattern) and long enough to go round the waist plus 5.5cm (2¼in).

ASSEMBLY

Inserting a semi-concealed zip

Zip insertion can be daunting. This method in a centre back seam is one of the easiest ways to start, as the centre back seam is straight – unlike a side seam, which is shaped. If possible, put the zip in before sewing the side seams. In addition, make sure you allow a minimum of 1.5cm (⅝in) seam allowance when sewing the

back seam (see the first step below).
It is difficult doing a good job with skimpy seam turnings.

1. Join the back seam, leaving a gap big enough to take the zip. Neaten the edges (see page 82), then press the seam and back opening into position.

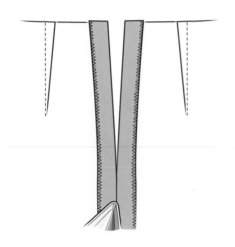

2. Pin and tack one side of the zip in place, aligning with the folded edge of one of the back opening seams, close to the teeth of the zip. Machine in place, stitching from the top of the zip down.

3. Pin and tack the other side of the zip into position so that the folded edge of the seam allowance covers the zip teeth and just covers the row of stitching you have just worked.

4. Before you machine the other side of the zip into position, place a narrow strip of masking tape at least 6mm (¼in) away from the fold and use this as a machining guide. Machine in place, stitching from the base of the zip to the waistband.

5. Remove the tape and tacking stitches

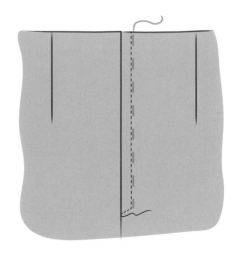

Drop in a lining!

This pattern doesn't include lining, but it's very easy to make. A lined garment feels so wonderful, draping well on the body.

1. Having cut out the lining (see page 231), tailor tack all the darts and seams as you did for your skirt. Don't reverse at the beginning of seams to secure threads when machining, as this screws up and tangles the edge of the fabric, being relatively fine and slippery.

2. Join the back seam before you sew the back darts. Why? Lining looks the same on both sides and once you separate the bits, it is so easy to make the darts the wrong way round!

3. Once you've sewn all the pieces together, cut 2.5cm (1in) off the hem edge – you need to do this so that the lining is slightly shorter than your skirt, hence not visible.

4. Drop the lining into your skirt with the wrong sides together. Pin the skirt and lining together at the waist and attach the waistband (see below) to both layers.

Waistband

This is a brilliant way to make a self-stiffening waistband. The fabric is folded over double – making the waistband more substantial than the one supplied in the pattern – and you wrap the waistband round the seam at the top of the skirt, giving it extra body.

1. Fold the strip in half lengthways, with wrong sides together, and press.

2. Place the folded band on the top of the right-hand side of the skirt, right sides together, with 1.5cm (⅝in) of the waistband projecting beyond the zip on one side and 4cm (1¾in) on the other end.

3. Pin, tack and machine in place 1.5cm (⅝in) away from the raw edge.

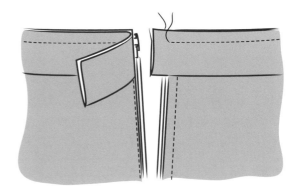

4. Press all seam edges up, so that the waistband projects above the top of the skirt, and fold over the end that overlaps the zip.

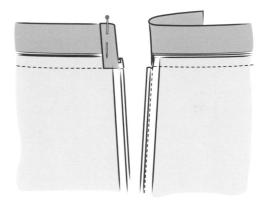

5. On the other end of the waistband you will have a projecting piece. Turn the very end under by 5mm (¼in) and press in place (see diagram overleaf).

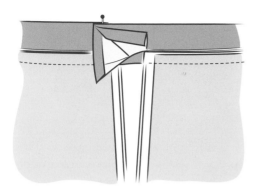

8. Slip-stitch both ends of the waistband to finish and attach a hook and bar for fastening the top of the skirt together.

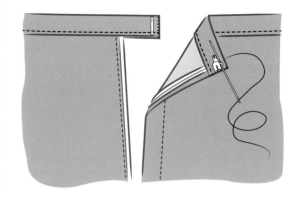

6. Fold the waistband over to the inside of the skirt so that the folded edge comes just below the row of machining holding the waistband. Press, pin and tack in position.

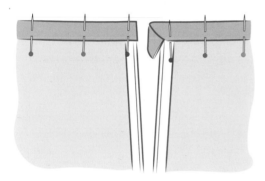

Invisible hem

For a truly professional finish to your skirt, I'd recommend sewing an 'invisible' hem by hand – one in which the stitching can't be seen on the outside of the garment. See page 86 for instructions on how to do this. The important thing is keep your stitches slack so that they do not pull on the right side of the skirt and hence become 'visible'.

7. Stitch the waistband on the right side of the skirt, just under the join – this is called 'stitching in the ditch'! This row of stitching will catch the lower edge of the waistband in place on the inside of the skirt.

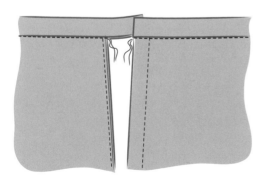

ADULTS' FASHION

ADULTS' FASHION

ADULTS' FASHION

BONED BODICE
Butterick B5419

Over the years I have made several boned bodices for my nieces. I have the joy of creating something special for a member of my family and we get to spend some quality time together. The bodice in the photo is made with silk purchased in a souk in Qatar. You can splash out on a really super piece of silk, as a bodice like this needs such a small quantity of fabric.

Don't be frightened of boning: think of it as just the scaffolding or support structure in a garment. There are lots of different types of boning. The easiest one for beginners to use is flexible plastic encased in its own cotton tape. The advantage of using this is that you can slip the boning out, attach the tape and then put the boning back in. In the pattern, the pieces of boning are attached to the seams of the lining, which is then joined to the main fabric. In my version of the bodice, I've incorporated the boning into an interlining of calico to give the garment extra body. I've also inserted the boning into the centre of each panel of the bodice rather than along the seams, which means that the boning sits flatter and there is less chance of the seams pulling.

Due to the boning, the bodice can be made strapless, as in the pattern. But the niece for whom I made the top wanted shaped straps that cross over at the back, partly to afford her the extra security she felt she needed and partly because they create such a lovely design feature. You could have straps that don't cross over, if you prefer, or you could substitute fine rouleau straps instead (see page 109).

YOU WILL NEED

Main fabric: 1m (1⅛yd) silk, 115cm (45in) wide
Lining: 1m (1⅛yd) polyester or acetate lining, 115cm (45in) wide
Interlining: 1m (1⅛yd) calico or cream-coloured polyester and cotton, 115cm (45in) wide (see tip on page 244)
Thread: All-purpose sewing thread
Accessories: 3m (3¼yd) length of 6mm (¼in) covered boning
30cm (12in) zip
Special equipment: Flexible curve ruler for marking the straps (optional)

CUTTING OUT

Bodice

Using the pattern pieces, cut your bodice out three times: once in the main fabric, once in the calico (see tip on page 240) and once in the lining. (It takes such a small quantity of fabric to make a bodice, I occasionally use the main fabric for lining.)

Straps

I cut my straps 60cm (24in) long and 12cm (4½in) wide, although the length of the straps will vary depending on the height of the person wearing the bodice. Use these dimensions to cut out two strips of silk, two pieces of lining and two pieces of interlining. (I used polyester and cotton curtain lining for the interlining, which has the advantage of being cream so that you can draw your shaping on to it.)

ASSEMBLY

Bodice

1. Pin and tack the calico pattern pieces together and fit on the person for whom you're making the bodice. Make any adjustments to this layer and make similar adjustments to the outer fabric and lining before you pin the pieces together.

2. Separate the calico pieces and attach the boning tape (this should be 1cm/½in longer than the boning) on to each of the panels on both sides (seven panels in total). The boning on the side and back panels should clear the top and bottom of the garment by at least 2.5cm (1in); the boning at the front of the bodice should start just below the bust, fitted to the person who will be wearing it. Machine-stitch along both long edges of the tape and 5mm (¼in) inside one short end. Insert the boning and machine across other end of the tape to stop the boning escaping.

3. Pin each of the calico pieces onto the wrong side of the main fabric, with the boning uppermost. Pin, tack and then machine the seams together, dealing with the calico and main fabric as one. Press the seams open and layer the edges (see page 82). Follow the pattern instructions for inserting the zip, attaching it to the combined main fabric and calico.

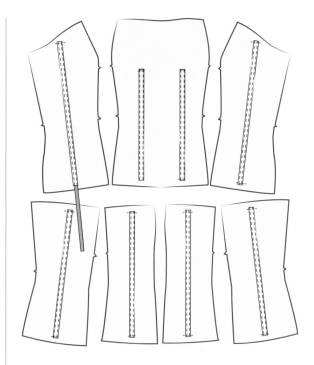

4. Join the lining pieces together and press the seams open, then follow the pattern instructions for attaching it to the main bodice.

Straps

1. First you need to shape each strap so that it tapers more at one end (for attaching at the back of the bodice). Using a ruler and a chalk pencil, draw two lines lengthways on the interlining, with a 3cm (1¼in) seam allowance on either side at one end narrowing to a 1cm (½in) allowance at the other. This is a guide only as these straps can be a size to suit; use a flexible curve ruler if you want curved shaping.

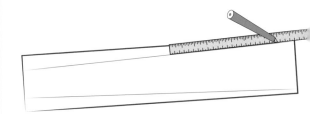

2. Next sandwich the silk between the interlining and the lining, with the silk and the lining placed right sides together and with the interlining on top, so that you can see the drawn lines.

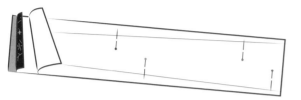

3. Pin, tack and machine all these layers together.

4. Insert a narrow cardboard tube (the tube from a roll of cling film is perfect) inside the strap. Press the seams open using the tube for support, then layer the seam edges.

5. Attach a large safety pin to the narrow end of the strap and turn through to the right side.

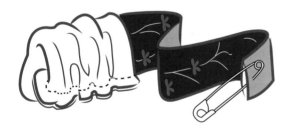

6. Press again, then repeat steps 1–5 to make the second strap.

Attaching the straps to the bodice

My bodice is cut straight along the top edge so it was easy to position the front straps and machine them into place. I inserted them so that they were square with the top edge of the bodice front and aligned with the bodice seams. The pattern I have recommended is shaped, however, and it is not as easy to get the straps in exactly the right place. I suggest you first finish the bodice and then attach the straps by hand on to the lining of the bodice at the end of construction. They will then be in exactly the right position and at the right angle, both back and front.

1. Fit the bodice with the person inside – the positioning and angle will be spot on. Pin each strap in the exact place that you wish to attach it, at the front and at the back of the bodice.

2. Remove the garment, then with the wrong side facing you, trim the ends of the straps so that you have 4cm (1½in) extending into the bodice. Fold under the ends of the straps by 1cm (½in) and slip-stitch the folded edges together.

3. Carefully slip-stitch the straps into position on the lining, making sure that your stitches do not puncture the silk on the outside of the garment. You may wish to sew round the end of each strap twice for security!

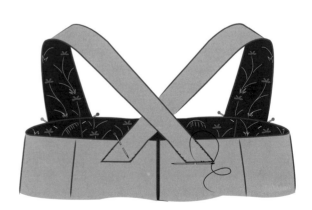

Calico is the traditional material for using in bodices, but it may shrink when washed. This won't be an issue, of course, if you intend to dry-clean your bodice, especially if it's made from an expensive piece of silk. Polyester and cotton lining would be preferable, though, if you want your bodice to be washable. In either case, a cream-coloured fabric is perfect for drawing the shaping of the straps. Cut out the calico pieces for the bodice first and add 2.5cm (1in) to each of the side seams to allow extra fabric for fitting.

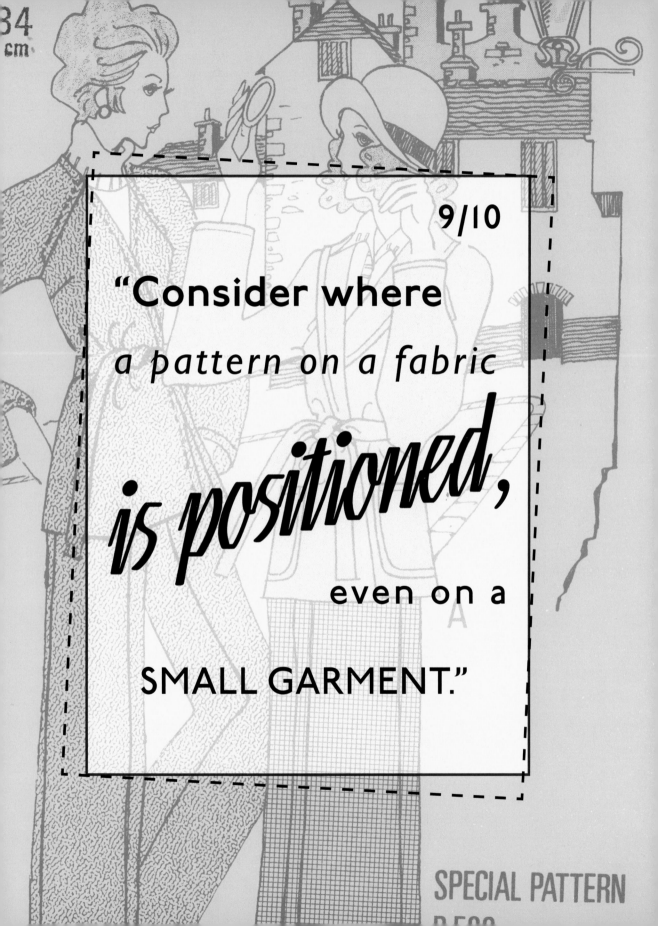

"Consider where *a pattern on a fabric* ***is positioned,*** even on a SMALL GARMENT."

ADULTS' FASHION

MAN'S WAISTCOAT
Vogue V8048

✕ ✕ ✕

Over the years I have made many waistcoats for the men in my family: tweed for my brother-in-law, velvet for my dad (two luscious burgundy and bottle-green velvet ones) and fine wool suiting for my husband, as he gets cold in the winter and a waistcoat helps keeps him warm beneath his suit. You could use silk, too, of course, or brocade. My students have gone a stage further, using fabrics depicting a loved one's hobby – from musical notes to fish!

YOU WILL NEED

(see the pattern for exact fabric requirements)
Fabric: 0.8–1m (⁷⁄₈–1yd) cotton or other fabric
    (see introduction), 115cm (45in) wide, or
    0.7–0.8m (¾–⁷⁄₈yd) cotton or other fabric,
    150cm (60in) wide
Interfacing: 1.3–1.4m (1³⁄₈–1½yd) fusible
    interfacing, 90cm (36in) wide
Thread: All-purpose sewing thread
Accessories: Four 16mm (⁵⁄₈in) buttons for
    covering (see page 112)

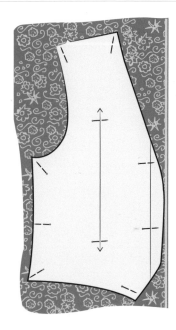

CUTTING OUT

Matching patterned fabric

I found this beautiful patterned cotton and thought it would be perfect for showing how to match a pattern.

1. Lay the fabric out in a single layer, right side up, in preparation for matching the two front sections of the waistcoat.

2. Place the waistcoat front pattern piece right side up on the fabric and pin in place, making sure that you align the grainline with the selvedge.

3. Cut this single piece out.

4. Mark the centre front, then remove the pattern piece.

5. Take the cut-out piece of fabric across to the other side of the length of laid-out fabric and position the piece right side up so that it overlaps the selvedge edge and aligns exactly with the patterned fabric underneath (see diagram overleaf).

6. Turn your paper pattern piece over so that the wrong side is facing you. Position the centre front of the paper pattern so that it covers the line drawn down the centre front on your cut-out piece of fabric.

7. Use a ruler to draw a line at right-angles to the selvedge, level with the lower point of the waistcoat. This will ensure that you position your paper pattern on the same level as the piece already cut out.

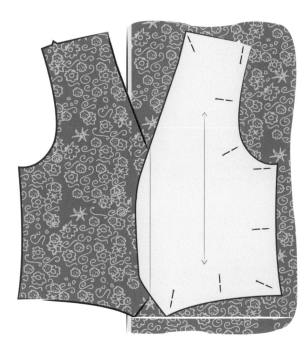

8. Pin the pattern piece into position except along the front edge.

9. Carefully lift up the pattern piece and remove the first cut-out front piece from underneath.

10. Pin the pattern piece along the centre edge and then cut out. You will now find that if you overlap the front left section over the right, you will have a perfect pattern match.

II. If using the same fabric for the back of the waistcoat, match the back section in the way, so that the design flows around the garment. Position on a double thickness of fabric with the centre back of the pattern piece along the fold. Alternatively, you could use a contrast fabric for the back.

ASSEMBLY

Follow the instructions in the pattern for assembling the waistcoat.

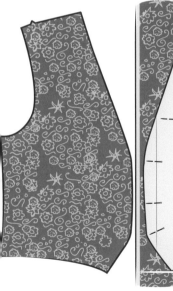

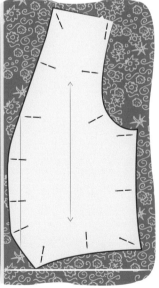

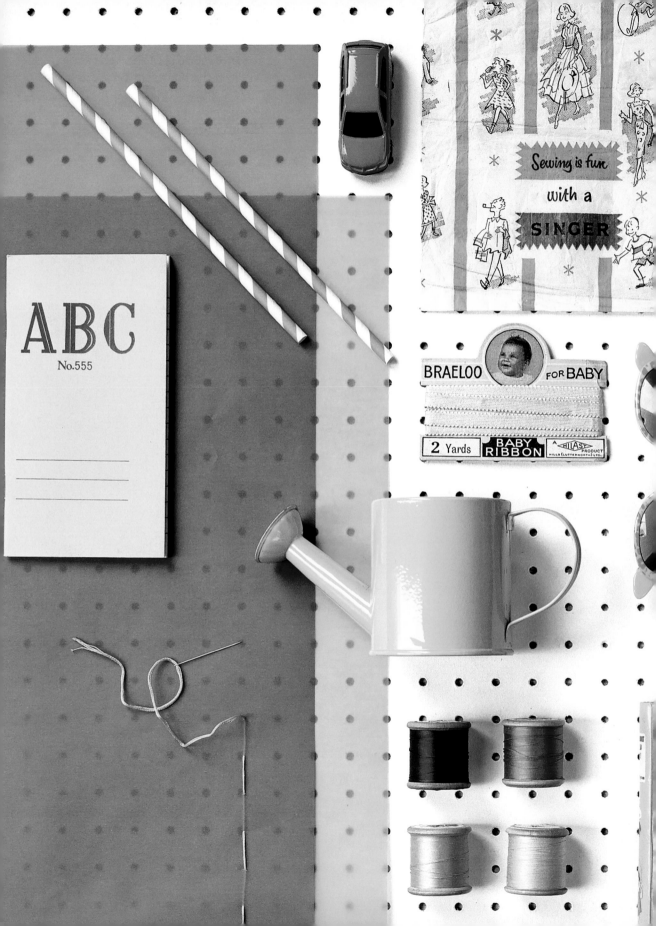

KIDS'
FASHION

KIDS' FASHION

JERSEY T-SHIRT
McCall's M4364

Sewing with cotton jersey can be challenging due to its stretchiness, but here I've suggested a few ways to help. And you don't necessarily have to buy a length of jersey for the T-shirt – why not recycle an adult one instead? There is a lot of fabric in an adult T-shirt, after all. I cut up a rather lovely bargain one in a great colour and made this fab child's T-shirt to coordinate with the shorts on page 252. I even used the hem on the adult T-shirt as the hem on my child's version – so easy!

YOU WILL NEED

(see the pattern for exact fabric requirements)

Main fabric: 0.5–0.7m (½–¾yd) cotton jersey, 150cm (60in) wide

Contrast fabric: 0.25–0.35 (¼–⅜yd) cotton or cotton jersey, 150cm (60in) wide

Thread: Polyester sewing thread

Needle: 75/11 stretch twin needle for the hems

Stabiliser options: 3mm (⅛in) clear stretch elastic for the shoulder seams, 1.3cm (½in) fusible stay tape, 0.5m (½yd) fusible interfacing (such as Vilene), double-sided 1.3cm (½in) fusible web (such as Lite Steam-A Seam) for the hems

CUTTING OUT

Cotton jersey

1. When laying the fabric out, it is almost impossible to get the cut edges to lie flat together. Match the selvedge edges (these have holes in them), stroking the fabric flat from the fold. If crosswise edges aren't even, cut these square using a gridded ruler as a guide.

2. When laying the pattern on the fabric, make sure that all the pieces are laid lengthways following the direction of the knit.

Recycling an adult T-shirt

Separate the front and back sections by carefully cutting along the side and top seams. Fold each in half down the centre line, matching the side seams together. Position the centre front of the T-shirt pattern on the fold of the front, aligning the bottom of the pattern with the bottom of the T-shirt so that the hem is incorporated, and do the same with the back section of the pattern/ T-shirt. Pin in place and cut out.

ASSEMBLY

Sewing seams

When making the seams on a sewing machine, use a small zigzag stitch (1mm/¹⁄₁₆in wide and 1mm/¹⁄₁₆in long). The extra 'give' in the stitch will allow the seam to stretch, whereas a straight stitch might snap with the strain.

If you have an overlocker, use a 6mm (¼in) three- or four-thread overlock stitch (see page 76).

If you do not have an overlocker, there are several stitches on a standard sewing machine that are perfect for sewing stretchy fabric (see page 65). If your machine has an over-edge, overcasting or overlocking foot (see page 56), it's best to attach this as it will have bars or brushes on it to help prevent the seam edge from puckering.

Stabilising seams and hems

My sample has sleeves and facing in standard cotton fabric that automatically stabilises the seams it is joined to, but if you're using cotton jersey for the whole garment, the following tips may help.

To help stabilise shoulder seams, pin a length of clear stretch elastic along each seam and machine through the three layers.

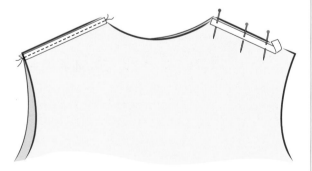

If you're binding the neckline (instead of attaching a facing), use fusible stay tape cut into short sections and apply these, overlapping, to the neckline to stop it stretching. Interfacing applied to facings also acts as a stabiliser.

To stabilise hemlines, iron fusible web along the hem edge of the garment. Peel off the paper, fold the hem over, press into position with a damp cloth for 10 seconds or until the adhesive has worked. Stitch with a stretch twin needle on the right side of the fabric.

KIDS' FASHION

TROUSERS & SHORTS

McCall's M4364

For many years I made both my sons Bermuda shorts in the summer and school shorts in the winter until it was deemed not cool to have a wardrobe made by your mum! With this pattern you have the option of making shorts/trousers elasticated or fastened with a drawstring. Either way, you make a casing at the top, which is ideal for finishing a waist on a child's garment, allowing room for growth so that you get maximum wear out of it. Combined with the T-shirt (see page 248), this pattern would also make a smashing pair of children's pyjamas.

YOU WILL NEED

(see the pattern for exact fabric requirements)
Fabric for the trousers: 1.15–2.4m (1¼–2⅝yd) cotton, 115cm (45in) wide, or 0.8–1.5m (⅞–1⅝yd) cotton, 150cm (60in) wide
Fabric for the shorts: 0.8–1.4m (⅞–1½yd) cotton, 115cm (45in) wide, or 0.8–1.05m (⅞–1⅛yd) cotton, 150cm (60in) wide
Thread: All-purpose sewing thread
Accessories: 0.8m (⅞yd) elastic 2cm (¾in) wide or 0.95–2.3m (1–2½yd) cording
2 drawstring stoppers (optional)

ASSEMBLY

When it comes to sewing them together, trousers can a bit of a mystery. My students frequently try and put the front leg flat on top of the back leg and wonder why it does not fit! The trick is to match the seams while making sure that you do not twist the legs. Here are a few tips based on using the pattern to make a very basic pair of shorts or trousers with simple hems (rather than casings for drawstrings) and no side pockets.

I. Place each front trouser leg on top of each back trouser leg, right sides together. Match the notches, then pin, tack and machine-stitch the inside leg seam. Repeat with the outside leg seams. Neaten the edges of the inside and outside seams using zigzag stitching (see page 65).

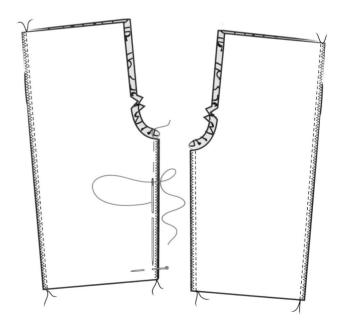

2. Turn one trouser leg right side out, then it slip inside the other trouser leg, which remains wrong side out.

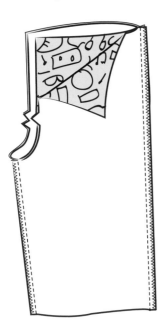

3. Match the crotch seams together, then pin and tack in place, machine together and neaten with a zigzag stitch, (See also tip, right.) Pull the inner trouser leg out so that both legs are now inside out.

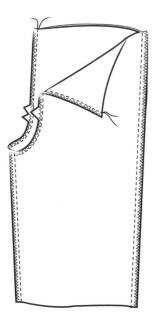

4. Make a casing at the waist (see section 3 in the pattern and page 102), following the pattern for inserting either elastic or a drawstring. Turn up and machine a small hem on each leg; see also tip below.

Machine the crotch seam again on top of the row you have just sewn. This strengthens the seam. Do the same on adult trousers. There is nothing more embarrassing than a crotch seam bursting!

Making casings and turning hems on children's clothes can be tricky because of their small size. Either press the seams using a sleeve board or insert a cardboard tube into the garment before ironing (see page 22).

10/10

"When cutting a small size

from a multi-size pattern,

use tracing paper

and a tracing wheel

TO MARK THE FITTING LINE –

then you still have the larger sizes

TO USE

as the child grows."

KIDS' FASHION

DUNGAREES

Kwik Sew K3948

These dungarees are fun to make and include a number of different techniques to extend your skills, including double topstitching (see page 64) and the option of adding appliqué details (see page 116). I've used a sturdy cotton for this project, although needlecord or a lightweight denim would work equally well. The pattern is easy to follow, but I've included a few additional notes to help you fashion really sharp-looking straps. You'll see I've also given instructions for making patch pockets with a contrast top edge.

YOU WILL NEED

(see the pattern for exact fabric requirements)
Main fabric: 0.95–1.15m (1–1¼yd) cotton, 106cm (42in) wide, or 0.7–0.95m (¾–1yd) cotton, 148cm (58in) wide
Contrast fabric: 0.25m (¼yd) cotton, 106cm (42in) wide
Binding: 1.85m (2yd) bias binding (to make your own, see page 104)
Thread: All-purpose sewing thread
Accessories: Four 15mm (⅝in) buttons
   2 buckle fasteners for the straps
   8–12 press fasteners

ASSEMBLY

Straps

The straps have a double-turned hem on each side. Here is a great tip to help you turn the hems and keep everything parallel. Creating a double hem on such a long narrow piece of fabric is much easier using this method, as you simply roll the turnings around rows of machine stitching, using them to guide the folds.

1. Follow the pattern up to the point in step 8 where you attach the strap to each back section of the dungarees, and then machine a row of stitching 5mm (¼in) from the outside long edge of the strap. Machine another row of stitching parallel to the first row and 8mm (⅜in) from the edge.

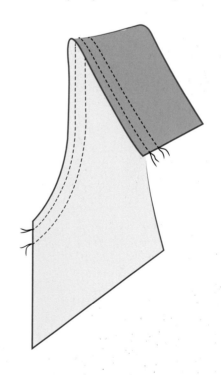

KIDS' FASHION

2. Fold over the first row of machine stitching so that the raw edge sits just short of the the second row and press.

3. Fold over the second row of stitching and press again.

4. Machine along the inner fold to hold the hem in place, then repeat for the other side of the strap.

5. You can also topstitch along the outer edge of each strap.

Pockets with contrast top edge

The pattern includes patch pockets, but you may like to make ones with a contrast top instead, as I've done for this project. My pockets are fully lined to hide all the untidy seam edges.

1. Cut one pocket piece from the main fabric to the size of the finished pocket plus a 6mm (¼in) seam allowance. This will be the front of the pocket.

2. Cut out a second pocket piece from the contrast fabric to the same size as the first piece but with a 2cm (¾in) seam allowance on the top edge. This will form the lining and contrast edge.

3. Place the two pocket pieces right sides together, aligning them along the top edge, and machine-stitch 6mm (¼in) from the top edge.

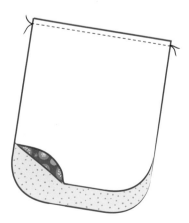

4. Press the seam allowance towards the top of the pocket. Align the bottom edges of the pocket pieces together, folding the surplus fabric at the top edge of the pocket so that it tucks in at the top edge.

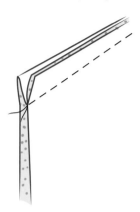

5. Machine down the sides and around the curved edge of the pocket, stitching 6mm (¼in) from the edge, holding the tuck in place at the top and leaving a 4cm (1¾in) gap in one side for turning the pocket through.

6. Clip the corners and trim the seams to 3mm (⅛in).

7. Turn the pocket right side out, inserting a point turner or chopstick through the gap to press out the seams. Slip-stitch the gap closed or catch in with the machine topstitching (see next step). Stitch along the bottom of the contrast edge.

8. Follow steps 1–7 to make the second pocket, then topstitch the pockets onto the back of the dungarees, stitching as close to the edge as possible. For extra strength you can put a small triangle of stitching at the top of each pocket edge, as for the double patch pockets on page 264.

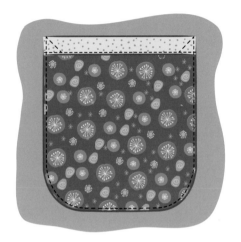

KIDS' FASHION

KIDS' FASHION

TODDLER DRESS
Butterick B5876

This is a really cute little dres that can be adapted in so many different ways, worn sleeveless on hot summer days or with a T-shirt underneath when it gets chillier. Here I've chosen to make the version with a contrasting band of fabric around the bottom and with patch pockets in the same fabric as the main part of the dress. I've used two different types of cotton – one patterned and one plain – but it could be made in a range of fabrics, depending on the time of year; denim or needlecord would work well.

YOU WILL NEED
(see the pattern for exact fabric requirements)

Main fabric: 0.6–0.7m (⅝–¾yd) cotton, 115cm (45in) wide, or 0.5m (½yd) cotton, 150cm (60in) wide

Contrast fabric: 0.6–0.8m (⅝–⅞yd) cotton, 115cm (45in) wide, or 0.5 (½yd) cotton, 150cm (60in) wide

Interfacing: 0.5m (½yd) length of fusible interfacing, 90cm (36in) wide

Thread: All-purpose sewing thread
Stranded embroidery thread

Needle: Crewel needle for sewing the button loop

Accessories: 7mm (⅜in) button

CUTTING OUT

Interfacing

I cut my interfacing slightly smaller than the facing – by about 5mm (¼in) – to reduce bulk on the hems and in the seams.

ASSEMBLY

Facings

This dress has a neck and armhole facing with a small, faced opening at the back. Follow the instructions in the pattern to join the front and back of the dress at the side seams and to join the front and back facings together at the side seams (up to the end of step 3 in the pattern), and then do the following (prior to pinning and sewing the facing to the dress):

1. On the wrong side of the back facing, mark the line that you will be sewing and cutting along for the opening. Neaten the lower edge of the facing: turn the edge of the facing under by 5mm (¼in), then press and machine-stitch along the folded edge on

the right side of the facing. It is much easier to stitch around curved hems that you have already pressed into position.

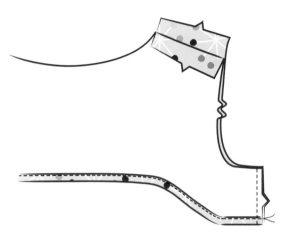

2. Place the facing and dress right sides together, matching the neck edge. Reduce the size of your machine stith so that, when you sew the back opening, it will be secure.

3. Starting from the shoulder on one side of the neck edge, machine-stitch along the neck edge and the marked line of the opening, working two small stitches at the base of the opening; this will make it much easier to turn through.

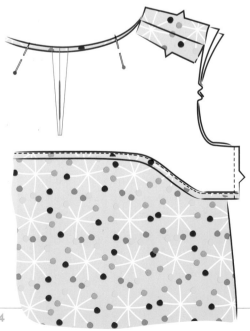

4. Snip along the line for the opening, clip and trim the neck seam (see page 84), then turn through to the right side and press the neck edge and opening (step 6 in the pattern). The extra trimming and clipping will ensure a nice crisp finish.

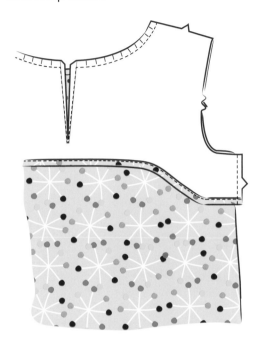

Double patch pockets

My preference is to make the pocket double so that you don't feel all the seam edges when you put your hands inside the pockets.

1. Cut out one pocket piece the finished size plus an extra 3cm (1¼in) on the top edge and a 1cm (½in) seam allowance around the rest of the pocket. This will be the outer pocket.

2. Cut out another pocket piece the finished size with a 1cm (½in) seam allowance all around. This will form the lining of the pocket.

3. Place both pocket pieces right sides together, aligning them along the top edge, and machine the top edge, leaving a 4cm (1¾in) gap in the middle of the seam.

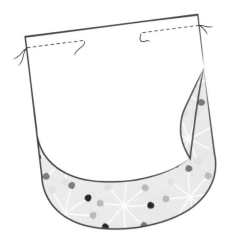

5. Attach both pockets to the bottom of the dress with edge stitching, keeping as close to the edge of the pocket as you can, and add a triangle of machining on the corners for extra strength.

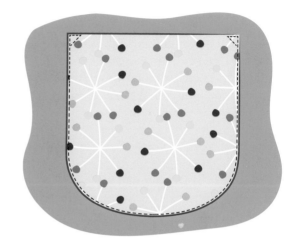

4. Press the seam open, then fold the pocket pieces right sides together, so that the seam comes partway down the back of the pocket, and machine the edges. Trim the seam edges to 3mm (⅛in) from the stitching, then turn through the gap in the lining. Use a point turner or chopstick to push the seams out. Press the pocket with the iron and slip-stitch the gap closed.Repeat steps 1–4 to make the second pocket.

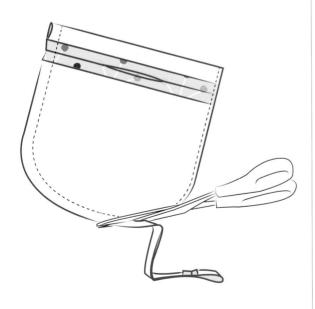

This is a great way to fasten the back of a garment – perfect for this little dress.

1. Thread a needle with 2–3 threads from an embroidery skein. Fasten the thread to the top of the back opening of the dress on the right-hand side and make a small loop, fastening this to the fabric about 5mm (¼in) below. (It's a good idea to check that your button fits comfortably through the loop before you fasten the thread to the other side.) Repeat back and forth to make a loop of six threads.

2. Work blanket stitch over this loop and fasten off the other end.

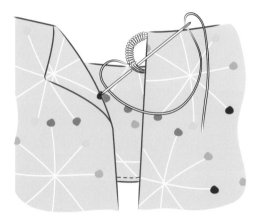

3. Sew the button onto the other corner of the opening.

Top Tip

For a perfect finishing touch, cover a button in a scrap of the patterned dress fabric (see page 112).

KIDS' FASHION

KIDS' FASHION

ROMPER SUIT

Kwik Sew K3983

X X X

This is a versatile pattern that you could use to make a little dress and trousers as well as the romper suit. I fell in love with this smashing jungle-print cotton, but you could use needlecord, gingham or denim and decorate with patterned cotton pieces following the instructions for appliqué on page 116. As the lion's head really stands out in the fabric I've chosen, it needs to be carefully positioned, which entails pattern matching. In order not to obscure the design, I haven't put pockets or any appliqué detail on the front of the romper suit, which means that the pattern on each side has to align properly. If you've chosen a fabric like this one with a prominent motif, do read the guidelines below before you start cutting out.

YOU WILL NEED

(see the pattern for exact fabric requirements)

Fabric: 1.2–1.4m (1¼–1½yd) cotton, 115cm (45in) wide, or 0.8–1.1m (⅞–1¼yd) cotton, 152cm (60in) wide

Interfacing: 0.2–0.3m (⅛–⅓yd) fusible interfacing 90cm (36in) wide

Binding: 2.2m (2¼yd) bias binding (to make your own, see page 104)

Thread: All-purpose sewing thread

Accessories: 2 x 15mm (⅝in) buttons 10 press fasteners

CUTTING OUT

Matching a patterned fabric

When positioning sections of a paper pattern on a patterned fabric, especially when the fabric has to be folded in half to make two identical pieces, you must match up dominant bits of the design first. You cannot simply match the selvedges when you fold, as the motifs may not be in the same place on both layers. Here, I matched the lion's head motif on the top piece of fabric with the same motif on the lower piece of fabric, pinning them together before attaching the paper pattern (the top part of the diagram overleaf shows the back of the pin on the lion's head, holding the bottom layer of fabric in place so that the lion's head will be in the same position in the centre when the two pieces are cut out.) In the photos on page 271, you can see that the lion's head appears in the centre of the yoke, on the back and the front, as well as along the centre of each leg.

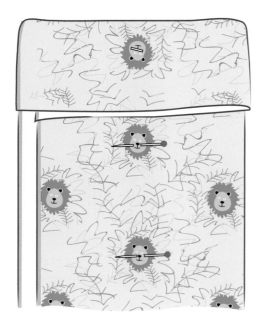

ASSEMBLY

Tucks

Step 2 of the pattern describes how to make two tucks at the top of each front leg piece before sewing them together. They need to be machined a little at the top. The following should help you to do this accurately:

1. Snip the seam allowance at the edge to mark where each tuck starts.

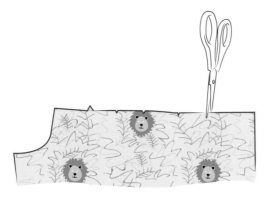

2. Fold the fabric right sides together to match these snips, then pin and tack ready for machining.

3. Either place the edge of the sewing-machine foot on the folded edge of the fabric and move the needle over to the left to align with the width of the tuck, or use the marking on the throat plate of the machine as a guide, then stitch to the point marked on the pattern.

4. Press the tucks flat to form little box pleats on the wrong side of the fabric. Stitch across the top of the pleats 1.5cm (⅝in) from the edge.

Curved seams

This pattern has several curved seams. For the best results, position the edge of the sewing-machine foot on the cut edge of the fabric and move the needle to the correct position to stitch. The edge of the fabric becomes a guide.

Pockets

For notes on double patch pockets, see the Toddler Dress (page 262).

KIDS' FASHION

KIDS' FASHION

SMOCKED DRESS

Butterick B3762

Smocking is proving to be very popular at the moment – it is a technique that my students keep asking to learn. Fabric is gathered into tubes or pleats and hand embroidery is used to hold these together. It is a really beautiful way of introducing shaping and fullness into a garment – soft fabrics such as cotton or silk will produce the best results. A wonderful project for those long winter evenings, smocking is very therapeutic and once you have mastered the basic technique, it is easy to pick up – to do a few stitches while you're watching TV, for instance – and put down again.

Here I have taken a classic high-waisted child's dress and incorporated a smocked section into the yoke. The dress in the photo is one I made my granddaughter some time ago for which the pattern is no longer available. However, the Butterick pattern I've recommended would work equally well as it is very similar in style and you could adapt the bodice in just the same way (see my instructions for cutting out on page 274). For the smocking I have included instructions here for two stitches that are easy to reproduce – cable and Vandyke – but there are many more to choose from, and different combinations can be used to striking effect. Pick a fabric with small checks such as gingham or a small spot design. Alternatively, use smocking dot transfer paper, which enables you to transfer dots onto the wrong side of the fabric ready for smocking. Either will give you an easy guide for the rows of gathering.

YOU WILL NEED

(see the pattern for exact fabric requirements for the dress)

Main fabric: 1.5–2.1m (1⅝–2¼yd) cotton or silk, 115cm (45in) wide, or 1.2–1.9m (1¼–2yd) cotton, or silk, 152cm (60in) wide

Fabric for smocked insert: 3–6 times the finished width of the smocked area – my dress used a piece 30cm (12in) wide for a finished insert of 8cm (3in). The amount of fabric needed will depend on the weight of the fabric and the type of stitches used. Do a test piece before you start.

Interfacing: 0.25m (¼yd) fusible interfacing, 90cm (36in) wide

Thread: All-purpose sewing thread (a good-quality thread is essential to ensure that your gathering stitches don't break)
Skein of embroidery thread in a bright contrasting colour

Needle: Crewel needle for the embroidery stitches

Accessories: Transfer paper for marking spots for the smocking (optional)
20cm (8in) zip

CUTTING OUT

Cut out the pieces of the dress following the pattern instructions. On the bodice front, mark out with pins or a chalk pencil the portion of the bodice that will be taken up by the smocking. (It's helpful to first mark the centre point of the bodice on the fabric to ensure that the smocked section is inserted symmetrically.) For a finished insert measuring 10cm (4in) wide, for instance, you would mark a section 8cm (3in) wide on the bodice – that is, 10cm (4in) minus 1cm (½in) for the seam allowance on each side. Cut out this portion of the bodice once you have done the smocking so that you can check the fit.

ASSEMBLY

Gathering

1. First neaten the top edge of the fabric for smocking with a narrow hem worked by machine or hand before you begin pleating the fabric. If using transfer paper, apply the spots to the fabric.

2. Next add rows of thread for gathering into pleats. I went across ten lines of spots on my fabric, catching each spot.

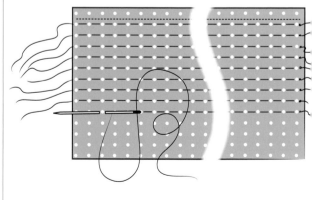

3. Form pleats in the fabric by carefully pulling the gathering threads and anchoring each end. This can be done by either tying the ends together in pairs (top left of diagram) or by winding the thread around a pin in a figure of eight (bottom left of diagram).

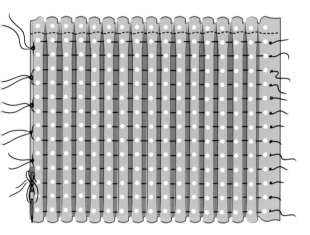

4. Make sure that the pleats are evenly adjusted across the fabric before you add your embroidery stitches.

Embroidering

1. Cut off a length of embroidery thread and gently pull the strands apart (there are six in total) to select the number that you'll need (2–3 strands). You can use the remaining strands for further stitching once you've used up the first length of thread.

2. Thread the crewel needle and work rows of your chosen embroidery stitch (see box, right, and page 276) across the pleats. Once you've completed the embroidery, you can pull out the gathering threads.

CABLE STITCH

This stitch is worked from left to right.

1. Bring your needle up on the first pleat. Holding the thread above the needle, pick up the next pleat horizontally and work a backstitch. Your stitch will go over two pleats.

2. Holding the thread below the needle, pick up the next pleat and work a backstitch so that your stitch goes over two pleats. Continue working stitches in the same way, with the thread alternately above and below the needle.

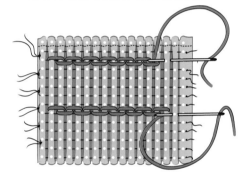

3. Double cable stitch is formed by working two rows of cable stitch close together. If the first row began with the thread looped below the needle, then the second row is started with the thread above the needle, or vice versa.

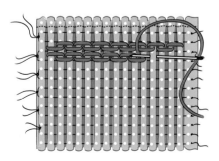

VANDYKE STITCH

This stitch is worked from right to left. It is very strong as the zigzag formation of the stitch makes it elastic.

I. Bring the needle up on the right side of the second pleat. Work a backstitch picking up the first and second pleats.

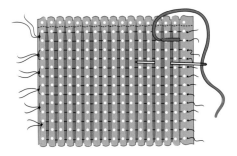

2. Move down this second pleat to the next row of gathering stitches and work a backstitch picking up this pleat and the next one. Make a backstitch across these two pleats.

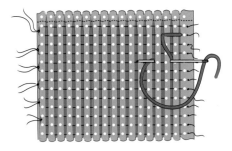

3. Move back up to the previous row of gathering and, on the same pleat, work a backstitch into this pleat and the next one.

4. Work stitches up and down these two lines of gathering stitches until you reach the end of the row.

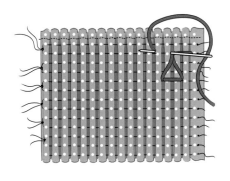

ASSEMBLING THE BODICE

Pin and tack the finished smocking insert to the front bodice sections, right sides together, and pin and tack to the other parts of the bodice to check the overall fit before machining together. Where the smocking attaches to the bodice front, you may need to adjust the seams a little before stitching in place by machine. (In my dress, for instance, the smocking tapers slightly from the top to the bottom of the bodice.)

KIDS' FASHION

CENTRE BACK

BACK
BUST 34
B590

LENGTHEN OR SHORTEN

×

TEMPLATES

*Unless otherwise stated, all templates are
actual size and include seam allowances.*

EXPRESS BUNTING
(page 136)

PRESSING TRIANGLE

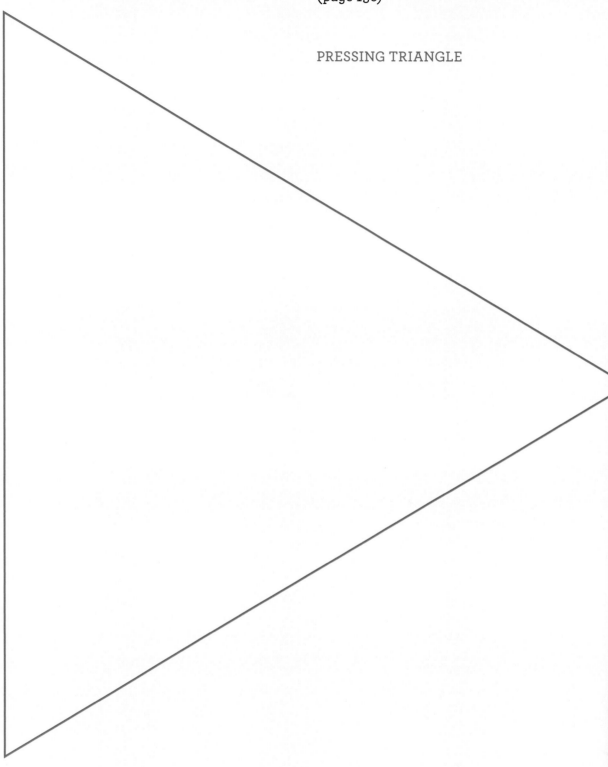

TEMPLATES

EXPRESS BUNTING

(page 136)

CHECKING TRIANGLE

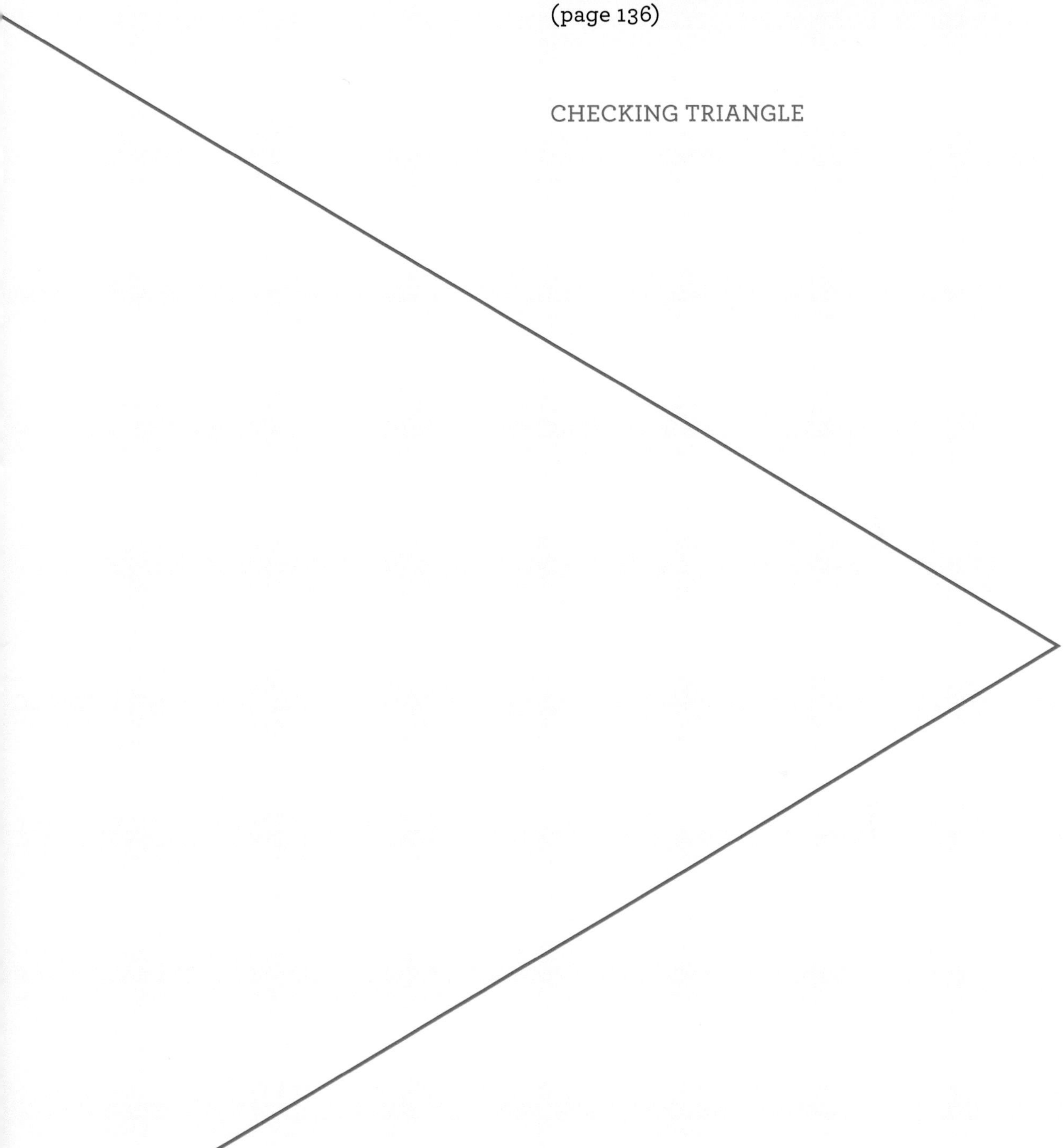

DOORWAY PUPPET
THEATRE
(page 140)

LETTERING

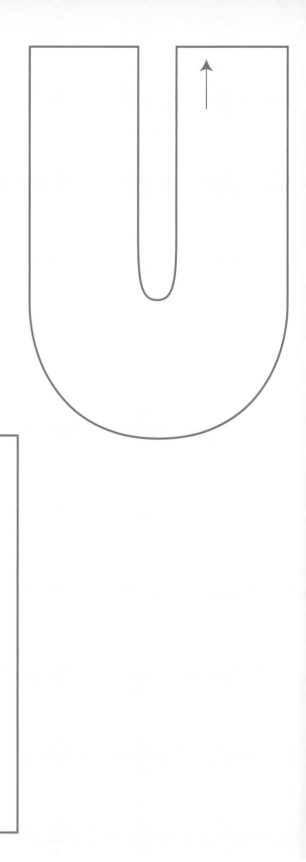

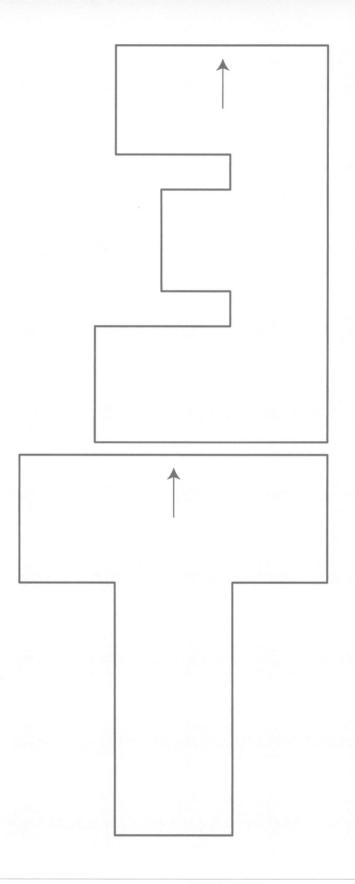

TEMPLATES

DOORWAY PUPPET THEATRE

(page 140)

LETTERING

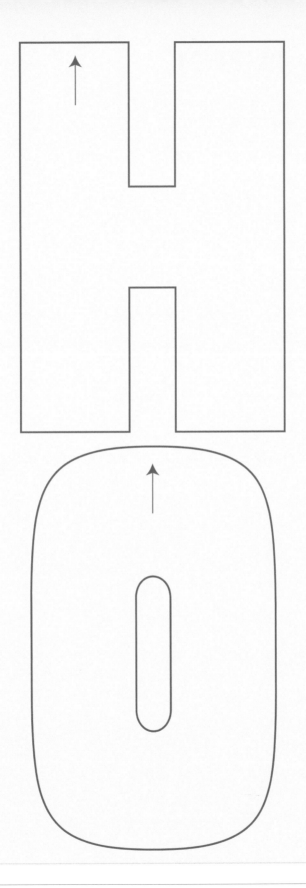

TEMPLATES

DOORWAY PUPPET THEATRE

(page 140)

SCALLOPED EDGE

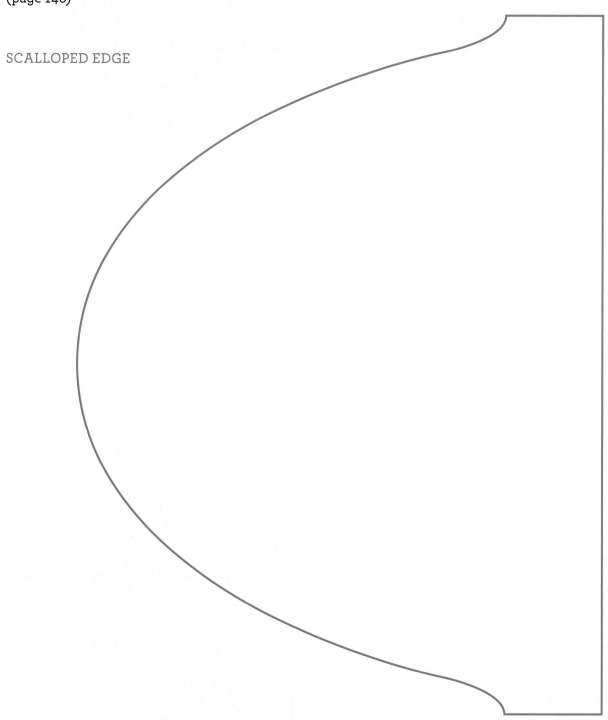

DOORWAY PUPPET THEATRE

(page 140)

BUNTING

HAND PUPPETS

(page 146)

Enlarge by 125%

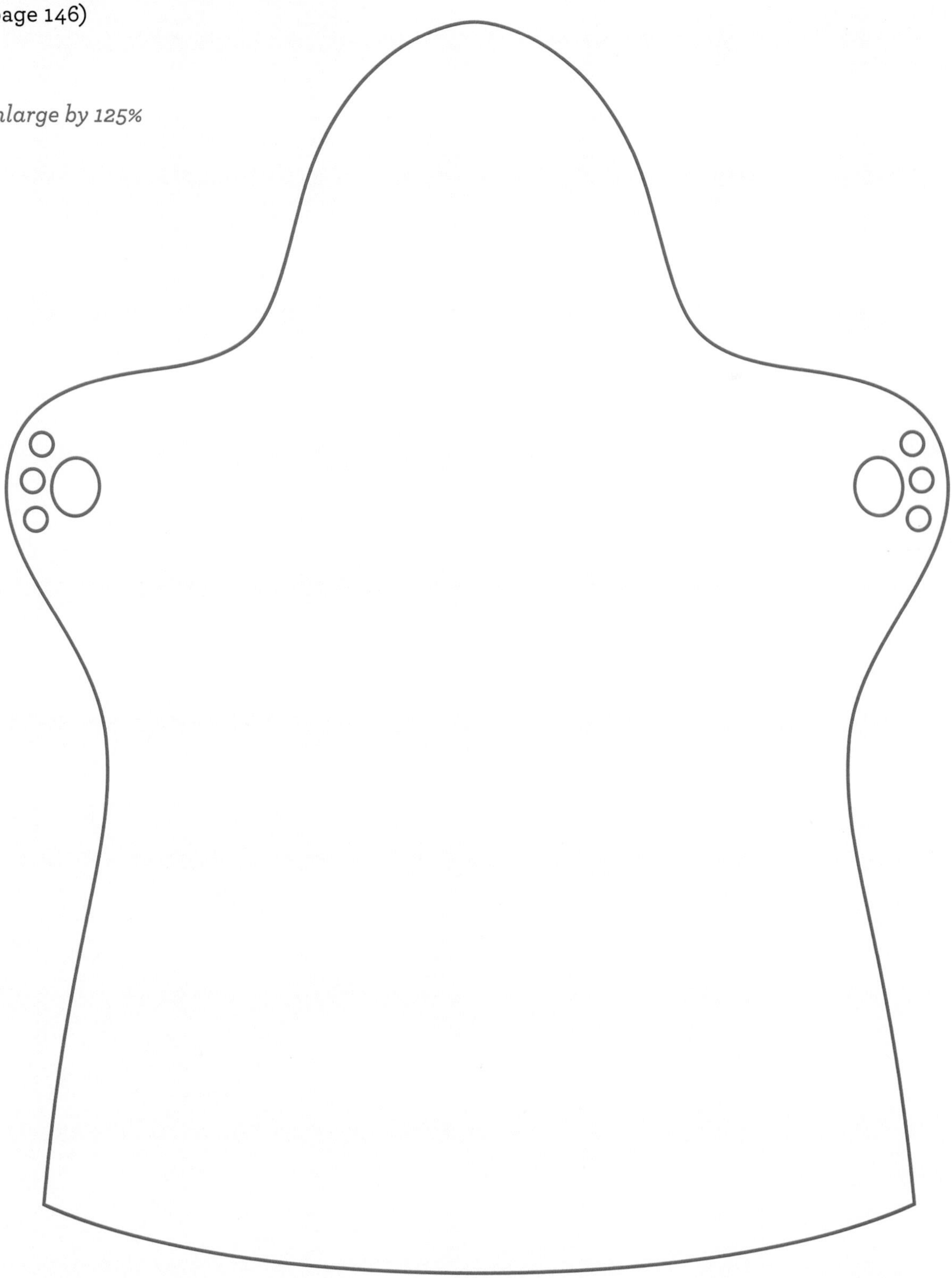

TEMPLATES

HAND PUPPETS
(page 146)

CITY MOUSE

TEMPLATES

HAND PUPPETS
(page 146)

SLEEPY MOUSE

OWL

OWL

CLOWN

TEMPLATES

CHRISTMAS STOCKING

(page 154)

Enlarge by 250%

TEMPLATES

PYRAMID BOX

(page 164)

HOLE TEMPLATE

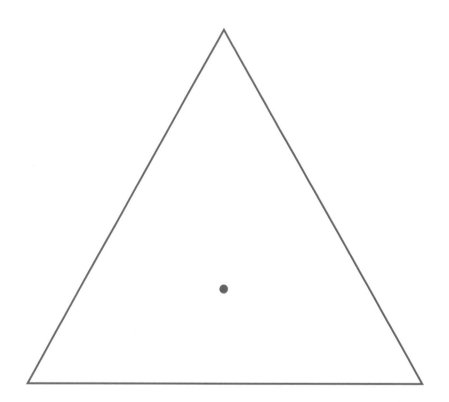

PYRAMID BOX

(page 164)

PIN CUSHION

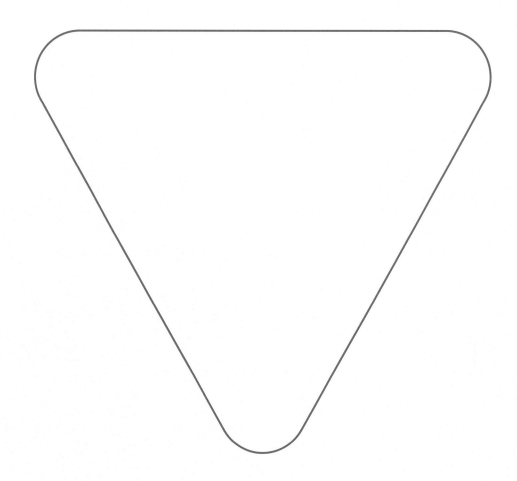

TEMPLATES

PYRAMID BOX

(page 164)

PYRAMID BOX OUTER

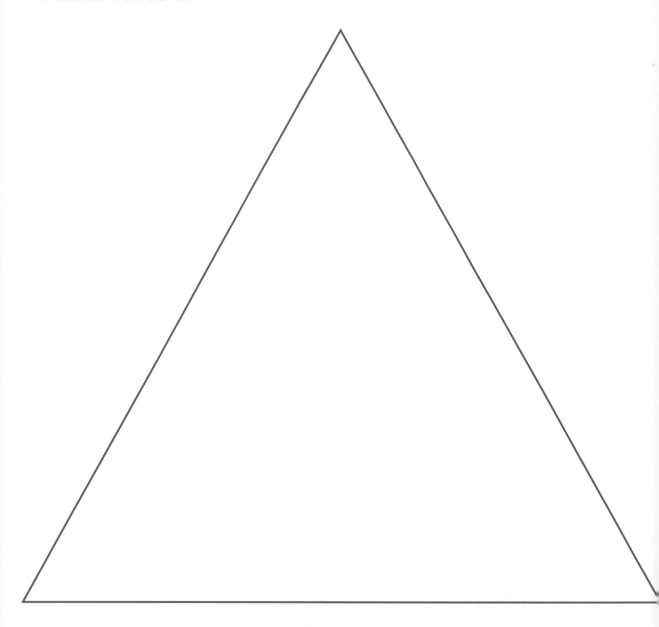

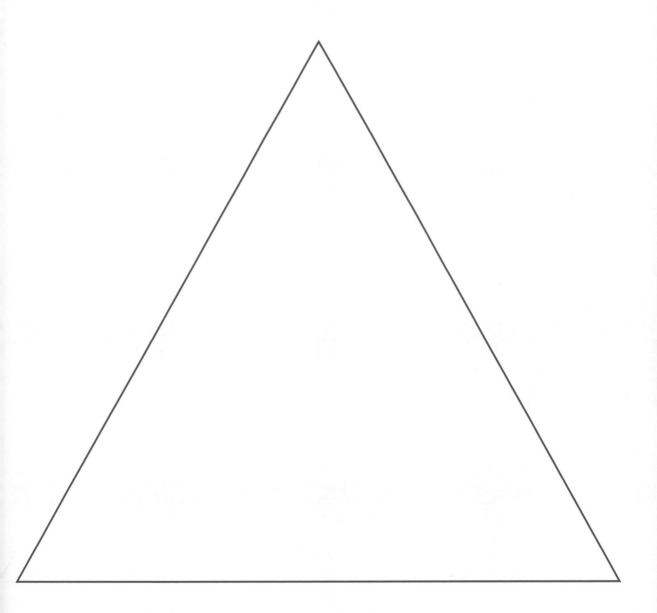

CHRISTMAS
DECORATIONS
(page 150)

HEXAGON STAR

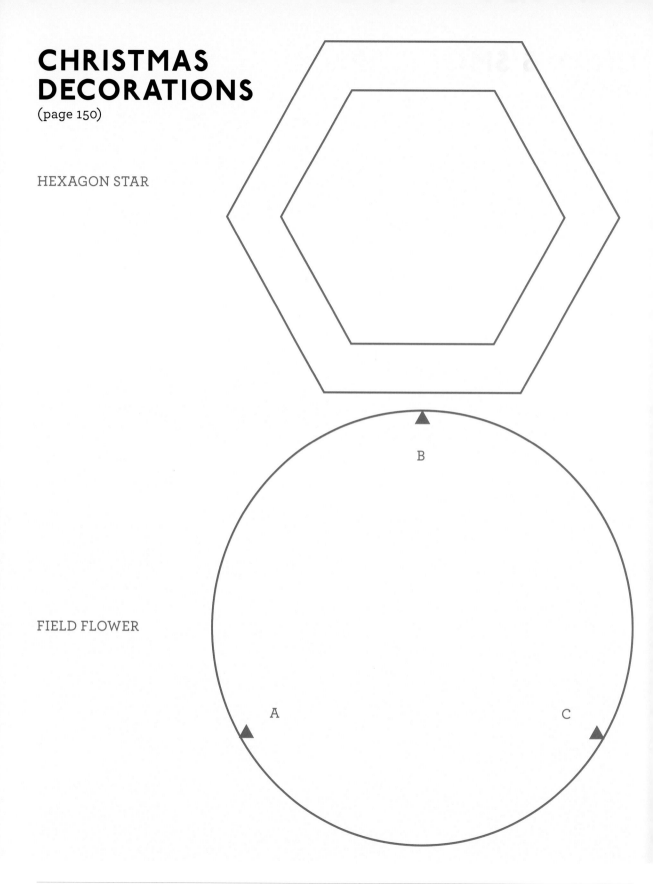

FIELD FLOWER

CHILD'S SMOCK APRON

(page 208)

CLOUD POCKET

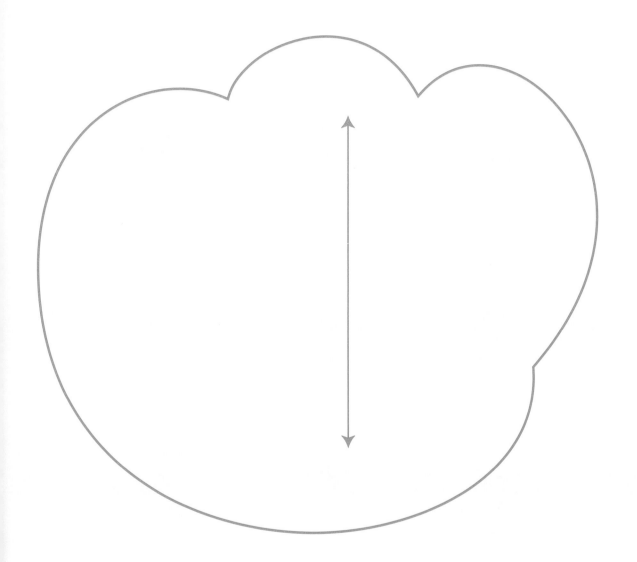

BUCKET BAG (page 216)

FRONT AND BACK, *Enlarge by 200%*

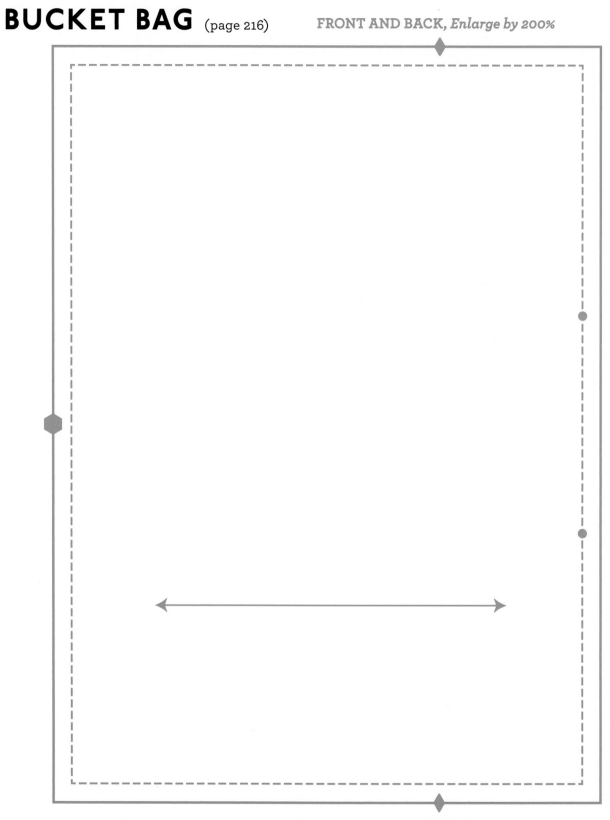

BASE,
*Enlarge by
125%*

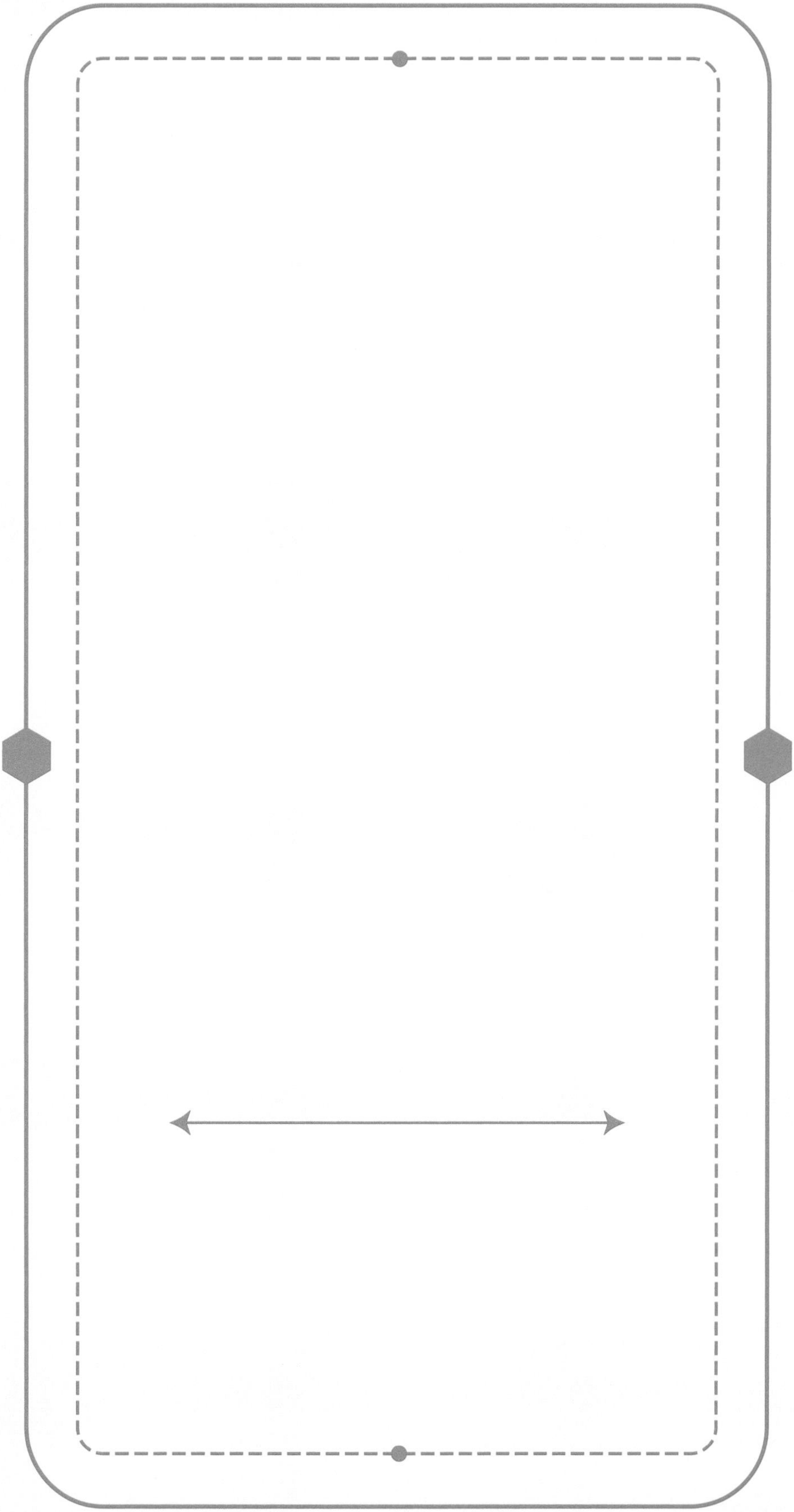

301

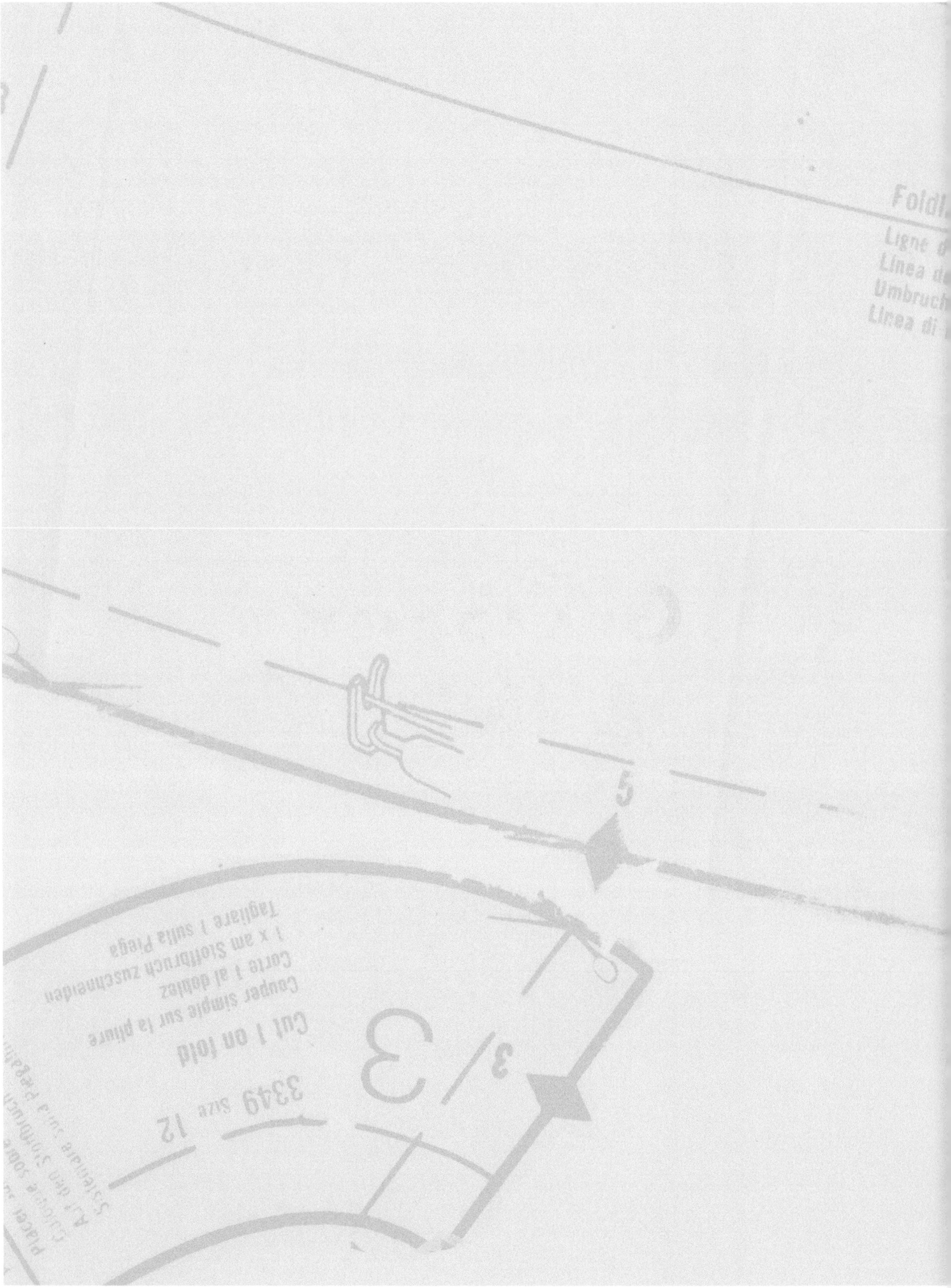

5

Tagllare 1 sulla piega

1 x am Stoffbruch zuschneiden

Carte 1 al doblez

Couper simple sur la pliure

Cut 1 on fold

3349 size 12

3

3/

×

GLOSSARY & INDEX

GLOSSARY OF SEWING TERMS

For more detail about specific hand stitches, including diagrams, see pages 50–51. For machine stitches, see pages 64–65.

✕ APPLIQUÉ

A decorative motif glued and/or stitched to the surface of a garment or other item.

✕ BACKSTITCH

A strong stitch with a double stitch on the wrong side. Good for repairing seams.

✕ BALANCE MARKS/POINTS

Marks on a paper pattern that are transferred to the fabric to provide reference points during construction.

✕ BASTING

Another term for tacking (see page 307).

✕ BIAS

At a 45-degree angle to the lengthways grain of the fabric. Cutting on the bias gives more stretch to the piece being cut out – necessary in binding a curved edge, for instance.

✕ BINDING

A narrow strip of fabric wrapped around the edge of a garment or other item to both neaten it and to look decorative. Bias binding consists of strips of fabric that are cut on the bias and joined together.

✕ BLIND HEMMING

A type of hem stitching worked by hand or machine. It is designed to be invisible on the right side of the garment, as the needle picks up only a couple of threads each time.

✕ BOBBIN

The small spindle on which thread is wound to provide the lower thread on a sewing machine.

✕ BUCKRAM

A type of stiffening generally used in curtain headings.

✕ CASING

A channel through which cord or elastic is drawn, such as at the top of a skirt or pair of trousers.

✕ CATCH STITCH

Large diagonal stitch used to finish hems.

✕ CREWEL NEEDLE

Needle with a long eye, used for embroidery.

✕ DART

A fold sewn in a garment to give shape to fit the contour of the body – for example, around the bust or waist.

× DRESSMAKER'S CHALK

Chalk, in the form of a triangle or pencil, used for marking details on fabric and for transferring markings from paper patterns.

× EASE STITCH

Longer running stitches made by hand or machine that are gathered slightly to help fit a longer edge of fabric, such as the top of a sleeve, into a shorter one.

× EDGE STITCH

Stitching worked close to the top folded edge of a seam or the edge of a garment to finish it.

× FACING

A shaped piece of fabric that echoes the area of the garment to which it is attached and to which it gives support.

× FAT QUARTER

A quilter's term based on the idea of a yard or metre of fabric cut into quarters like a sandwich. Each of these is a 'fat quarter'.

× FEED DOGS

Rows of little 'teeth' in a sewing machine or overlocker that move the fabric into position for each stitch.

× FITTING LINE

The line inside a pattern piece that is usually 1.5cm (⅝ inch) inside the cut edge. It is the line along which the garment pieces are joined together.

× FLAT FELL SEAM

A seam with a folded edge of fabric that is stitched down on the right side of the garment, such as on a pair of jeans.

× FUSIBLE

Referring to the surface of interfacing when it can be ironed onto fabric, the heat of the iron releasing the glue on the surface so that it fuses with the fabric.

× FUSIBLE WEB (PAPER-BACKED)

A fine layer of glue supported by a layer of silicone paper that can be ironed onto fabric and the paper peeled away for appliqué or garment repair.

× FRENCH SEAM

A seam traditionally used on lingerie. It is sewn twice – once to the right side and once to the wrong side – enclosing the raw edges.

× GATHER

Long running stitches that are worked by hand or machine and pulled up to create a frill or ruffle. Also used in smocking, the embroidery stitches being worked over the gathered surface of the fabric.

× GRAIN

The grain is created when fabric is woven. The grain parallel with the selvedge is the warp; the grain across the width of the fabric is the weft.

× GRAIN LINE

Line marked on a paper pattern to show the direction of the grain. This line should be parallel to the selvedge edge of the fabric.

INTERFACING

Support material of varying weights used between the main fabric and a facing. It comes in either sew-in or fusible (see above) forms.

INTERLINING

Fabric used as additional layer of support between the lining and main fabric of a curtain or garment.

LADDER STITCH (EVEN SLIP STITCH)

Stitch made by hand to join two folded edges; when the threads are pull apart slightly, they look like the rungs of a ladder.

MITRE

Neatened corner made where two hems meet; typically used on rectangular/square items like a curtain or napkin.

NAP

Fabric with a textured surface, pile or a printed one-way design. All pattern pieces should be placed in the same direction on the fabric.

NEATEN A SEAM

To finish the raw edges of a seam once it has been sewn, either with a narrow hem or by binding or oversewing the edges.

NOTCH

Either (a) a small section sticking out of the seam allowance on a paper pattern as a reference point; or (b) a small piece cut in the seam allowance at intervals along a convex curving edge to reduce bulk.

OVERLOCK

A type of looped stitch made by overlocker or sewing machine along the edge of a seam to neaten it or join it to another piece of fabric.

OVERSEW

Stitching, such as zigzag or overlock, taken over the edge of fabric to prevent it fraying or to join it to another edge.

PIPING

Narrow cord covered by binding and incorporated in a seam to give a decorative effect to the edge of a cushion or garment.

RAW EDGE

Cut edge of fabric that may fray or unravel unless it is neatened by hemming or oversewing.

RUNNING STITCH

A basic straight stitch made by hand or machine for joining seams, mending, tucking and gathering.

SEAM ALLOWANCE

The narrow strip between the line of stitches joining a seam and the edge of the fabric.

SELVEDGE

The neatened edge on a length of fabric. A roll of fabric has one on each long edge to prevent it from fraying. It is parallel to the warp grain.

× SLIP STITCH

Hand stitch used for securing hems that are folded over twice. The needle is taken through the folded edge and picks up a couple of threads from the fabric underneath so that it is scarcely visible on the right side of the article being hemmed.

× STITCH IN THE DITCH

A line of stitching made close to a seam allowance or in the seam itself.

× STAYSTITCH

A row of machine stitching worked in the seam allowance about 3mm (⅛in) from the fitting line.

× TACKING

Hand stitches that attach a seam temporarily before it is machined together.

× TAILOR'S TACK

A loose, looped stitch used to transfer markings, such as the location of a dart, from a paper pattern to the fabric.

× TOPSTITCHING

A row of running stitches worked by machine on the right side of the garment both for functional reasons, such as holding a facing in place, and to give a decorative finish.

× SPOOL PIN

The post on a sewing machine where a cotton reel is placed to provide the upper thread.

× THROAT PLATE

The metal plate on a sewing machine below the presser foot. It has a hole in it through which the needle passes as it stitches and over which the fabric is fed.

× TURNING OUT

Turning a garment or other item the right way out when the seams have been sewn together.

× UNDERSTITCHING

A row of machining worked on the edge of a facing next to the seam attaching the facing to the garment.

× ZIGZAG

Stitching made by machine to neaten the raw edges of a seam, sew stretchy fabric together (where straight stitching might break), make a buttonhole or create decorative effects.

INDEX

MY LITTLE BLACK BOOK

Gone are the days when every single town, no matter how small, had its own draper's shop and you could while away the hours perusing paper patterns, pulling out rolls of fabric, and sifting through drawers of ribbons, buttons and trims to find the perfect embellishment. Thankfully, there are still lots of shops around the country with knowledgeable staff ready to help you. And, of course, the rise of the Internet has transformed the way we shop: at the click of a mouse, you have access to fabrics and trimmings from all over the globe. However, I do think you need to hold and feel a fabric before you buy it so, even if I'm buying online and can't hold up the whole roll to check how it drapes, I always try to get hold of a sample of the fabric I'm interested in – particularly as it's impossible to get a refund on cut fabric if you don't like it when it arrives.

Here are some of my favourite shops and sites; note that most of the physical shops also sell online.

✕ FABRIC SHOPS

1st For Fabrics Ltd
Unit 9B
North Tyne Industrial Estate
Benton
Newcastle Upon Tyne NE12 9SZ
Tel: 0191 270 1333
www.1stforfabrics.co.uk
Carries an enormous selection of both dressmaking and soft-furnishing fabrics.

C&H Fabrics
www.candh.co.uk
Has nine shops in the south-east of England, stocking fabric for clothes and soft furnishings, haberdashery and much more.

Calico & Co
www.calicoandco.com
Extensive range of designer dressmaking and soft-furnishing fabrics. Shops in Cardiff and Bristol.

Cloth House
47 Berwick Street
London W1F 8SJ
Tel: 020 7437 5155
www.clothhouse.com
Specialises in cotton and linen fabrics.

Cloth House
98 Berwick Street
London W1F 0QJ
Tel: 020 7287 1555
www.clothhouse.com
Stocks silks, jersey, wools, prints and unusual fabrics.

Edinburgh Fabrics
12–14 St Patrick Square
Edinburgh EH8 9EZ
Tel: 0131 668 2790
www.edinburghfabrics.co.uk

Fabrics Galore
52–54 Lavender Hill
London SW11 5RH
Tel: 020 7738 9589
www.fabricsgalore.co.uk
Has an excellent range of fabrics from around the world; supplied fabrics for The Great British Sewing Bee.

Fabric Land
www.fabricland.co.uk
A fantastic selection of fabric and haberdashery to suit every pocket. Has nine shops in the south of England.

Greenhill Patchwork and Quilting
3 Bell Street
Romsey
Hampshire SO51 8GY
Tel: 01794 517973
www.greenhillpatchwork.co.uk
An Aladdin's cave of patchwork and quilting supplies.

Hansons Fabrics

Station Road
Sturminster Newton
Dorset DT101BD
Tel: 01258 472698
www.hansonsfabrics.co.uk
Brilliant range of fabrics for dressmaking and patchwork, craft supplies, sewing machines and equipment.

MacCulloch and Wallis

25–26 Dering Street
London W1S 1AT
www.macculloch-wallis.co.uk
An established shop not far from London's Oxford Street, excellent for all your sewing fabrics, linings and interfacings.

Mandors

131 East Claremont Street
Edinburgh, EH7 4JA
Tel: 0131 558 3888
0131 556 8777
www.mandors.co.uk

Mandors

134 Renfrew Street
Glasgow, G3 6ST
Tel: 0141 332 7716 (dressmaking) and
0141 332 4221 (curtains)
www.mandors.co.uk

Masons Fabrics Shop

20 Bath Street
Abingdon
Oxon OX14 3QH
Tel: 01235 527720

Masons Craft Shop

22 Bath Street
Abingdon
Oxon OX14 3QH
Tel: 01235 520165

Masons Upholstery Shop

39 Stert Street
Abingdon
Oxon 0X14 3JF
Tel: 01235 520107
www.masonsneedlecraft.co.uk
Three brilliant shops in Abingdon Oxfordshire great for all your sewing needs.

Simply Fabrics

57 Atlantic Road
London SW9 8PU
Tel: 020 3602 0723
www.simplyfabrics.org.uk
Specialises in sourcing remnants from garment factories; there may be designer pieces in the mix! Supplied fabrics for The Great British Sewing Bee.

Stone Fabrics

97 High Street
Totnes
Devon TQ9 5PB
Tel: 01803 868608
www.stonefabrics.co.uk
An impressive range of fabrics and haberdashery.

Truro Fabrics Store

Lemon Quay
Truro
Cornwall TR1 2LW
Tel: 01872 222130
www.trurofabrics.com

✕ FOR TRIMMINGS AND HABERDASHERY

The Button Queen

76 Marylebone Lane
London W1U 2PR
Tel: 020 7935 1505
www.thebuttonqueen.co.uk
Specialises in (surprise, surprise!) buttons.

Duttons for Button

www.duttonsforbuttons.co.uk
Has stores in York, Harrogate and Ilkley and, contrary to the name, sells ribbons, trimmings and an extensive range of zips and other haberdashery items, as well as buttons.

Kleins

5 Noel Street
London W1F 8GD
Tel: 020 7437 6162
www.kleins.co.uk
Sells all kinds of haberdashery items, including interesting trimmings.

Simply Fabrics
48 Atlantic Road
London SW9 8JN
Tel: 020 7733 2877
www.simplyfabrics.org.uk
The trimmings and haberdashery branch of the fabric store listed above.

V V Rouleaux
102 Marylebone Lane
Marylebone
London W1U 2QD
Tel: 020 7224 5179
www.vvrouleaux.com
The Rolls Royce of Ribbons! Also sells every kind of braid, cord and fringing imaginable.

✕ ONLINE SITES

Acorn Fabrics
www.acornfabrics.com
Good for shirting fabrics.

Backstitch
www.backstitch.co.uk
Really great patterns and fabrics.

Butterick Patterns
www.sewdirect.com
Patterns to suit all levels of sewing ability.

The Cotton Patch
www.cottonpatch.co.uk
Great for patchwork fabrics and quilting supplies.

Fabric Loft
www.thefabricloft.co.uk
Designer fabrics, haberdashery and paper patterns.

McCall's Patterns
www.sewdirect.com
Patterns to suit all levels of sewing ability.

Sewbox
www.sewbox.co.uk
For fabrics, patterns and haberdashery.

Sewdirect
www.sewdirect.com
Sells paper patterns at a fraction of the shop price.

Simplicity Ltd
www.simplicitynewlook.com
Patterns to suit all levels of sewing ability.

Thread and Loop
www.threadandloop.co.uk
Fantastic supplies for all soft furnishings at good prices.

Tissu Fabrics
www.tissufabrics.co.uk
Particularly good for stretch fabrics.

✕ FOR THE BUDDING TEXTILE DESIGNERS AMONG YOU

Fabric Press
www.thefabricpress.com
A digital printing service that enables you to have your own images and designs made up into cotton fabric.

Spoonflower
www.spoonflower.com
Design your own fabric and they print it – on a range of 15 fabrics, including silks, organic cottons and a linen blend.

✕ FOR SEWING MACHINES AND OTHER EQUIPMENT

Bernina
www.berninaukshop.co.uk
Quality sewing machines.

Creative Grids
www.creativegrids.com
Specialises in gridded rulers, cutters and mats, but also sells wadding and threads.

Jaycotts
www.jaycotts.co.uk
A really good online store for sewing machines, tools and gadgets, and storage, as well as haberdashery.

Sewing Machines Direct
www.sewingmachine.co.uk
Fantastic range of sewing machines and brilliant service.

ACKNOWLEDGEMENTS

I would like to thank the following people who have helped me along the way:

My wonderful family for all their support while I was writing this book – in particular, my sister Jean, who came to meetings and made sense of some of my text.

My husband David for his boundless support and encouragement.

Greenhill Patchwork and Quilting shop in Romsey for their generosity in supplying all the fabrics for the projects in this book.

Prym, who supplied me with a selection of gadgets and haberdashery.

Sewing Machines Direct, who supplied me with a sewing machine and attachments for the photography.

At HarperCollins, Vicky Eribo and Georgina Atsiaris got the project off the ground and Lucy Sykes-Thompson designed a book that is both stylish and informative. Sarah Hoggett and Kate Parker went through the text with a fine-tooth comb, while Kate Simunek and Stephen Dew turned my rough sketches into beautifully accurate illustrations. My thanks, too, to photographer Ali Allen, stylist Alice King, hair and make-up artist Sarah Matheson, proofreader Marie Clayton and indexer Marie Lorimer.

ACKNOWLEDGEMENTS

HarperCollins*Publishers*
77–85 Fulham Palace Road,
Hammersmith, London W6 8JB

www.harpercollins.co.uk

First published by HarperCollins*Publishers* 2014

10 9 8 7 6 5 4 3 2 1

Sewing pattern illustrations reproduced by kind permission
of Simplicity Patterns (p. 197, p. 203, p. 255); Butterick Patterns
(p. 66, p. 93); IPC (p. 29, p. 123, p. 241)

Every effort has been made to contact the copyright holders but
the publishers would be glad to hear of any omissions.

A catalogue record of this book is available from
the British Library

ISBN   978-0-00-757304-2

Printed and bound at Printing Express, Hong Kong

Designer: Lucy Sykes-Thompson
Illustrators: Stephen Dew and Kate Simunek
Photographer: Ali Allen
Stylist: Alice King
Hair and Make-up Artist: Sarah Matheson